Solo Guitar Playing

FOURTH EDITION

Solo Guitar Playing

Book

Frederick M. Noad

Exclusive Distributors:
Hal Leonard
7777 West Bluemound Road
Milwaukee, WI 53213
Email: info@halleonard.com

Hal Leonard Europe Limited
42 Wigmore Street
Marylebone, London, W1U 2RN
Email: info@halleonardeurope.com

Hal Leonard Australia Pty. Ltd.
4 Lentara Court
Cheltenham, Victoria, 3192 Australia
Email: info@halleonard.com.au

Editorial Advisor: John Schneiderman
The three photographs illustrating playing positions are by Bevis/Toledo;
the remainder are by James Shade.

Printed in the EU

Contents

LESSON ONE
Basic Technique

LESSON TWO
Right Hand Techniques

CONTENTS

LESSON THREE
Beginning to Read Music

LESSON FOUR
Notes on the Frets

LESSON FIVE
Notes, Rests, and Ties

LESSON NINE
Introduction to Chords

LESSON TEN
Music in Two Lines

LESSON ELEVEN
Ligado Techniques

LESSON TWELVE
Dotted Notes

LESSON THIRTEEN
The Second Position

LESSON FOURTEEN
Musical Indications

LESSON FIFTEEN
The Third Position

LESSON SIXTEEN
New Time Signatures

LESSON SEVENTEEN
The Fifth Position

LESSON EIGHTEEN
The Full Bar

LESSON NINETEEN
Scales

LESSON TWENTY
Melody and Arpeggio

LESSON TWENTY-ONE
Ornamentation

LESSON TWENTY-TWO
The Seventh Position

LESSON TWENTY-THREE
Contrapuntal Music

LESSON TWENTY-FOUR
Harmonics

LESSON TWENTY-FIVE
Advanced Techniques and Effects

LESSON TWENTY-SIX
Completion of the Fingerboard

APPENDIX
Music for Guitar Ensemble

Additional Repertoire
from *The Frederick Noad Guitar Anthology*

Preface to the Fourth Edition

It is an honor to be editorial advisor for the fourth edition of *Solo Guitar Playing*, a book used by hundreds of thousands of guitarists worldwide. I have been studying and teaching from *Solo Guitar Playing* since its first printing in 1968.

I had the good fortune of having Frederick Noad as my guitar and lute teacher from 1974 through 1978. It was during this period that he transcribed much of the repertoire for *The Frederick Noad Guitar Anthology*, and my lessons frequently involved sightreading/proofreading.

The revisions to the fourth edition have been non-invasive. A number of notational mistakes have been corrected and a selection of repertoire gleaned from *The Frederick Noad Guitar Anthology* has been added.

For those of you already familiar with *Solo Guitar Playing*, I hope you enjoy the additional repertoire, and for those of you new to the book, you are in for a treat.

John Schneiderman
Orange, California, June 2008

Preface to the Third Edition

Once again, I am happy to have the opportunity to add to *Solo Guitar Playing*, and also to make some changes where my own use of the book and the helpful comments of other teachers have suggested possible improvements. In some cases, time has revealed better fingerings, and in others, improvements have been made to exercises to make them more musically satisfactory while retaining their specific teaching purpose.

In the beginning lessons, I have added material to give extra practice to the notes below the staff, a weak area for many new students, including more interaction between bass and treble as opposed to melodic lines confined to one or the other. I have added to the early repertoire for the same reason.

On a more advanced level, I have increased the exercise and duet material related to learning the higher positions, and have also added to the performance solos that use these positions. I believe that this makes for an easy transition to Book II without any feeling of added difficulty.

To the appendix of ensemble pieces for class use, I have added some favorites of proven success, in particular the highly accessible and rewarding original works for three guitars by the early nineteenth-century romantic Leonhard von Call. Extremely easy to play, I have found these trios to be a popular success with guitar classes and helpful in instilling that sense of ensemble playing and accurate time-keeping so often lacking in students with primarily soloist ambitions.

In conclusion, I should like to thank the many teachers who have generously shared their comments and suggestions and hope that they will enjoy recognizing their contributions to this enlarged edition.

Preface to the Second Edition

The response to the initial edition of *Solo Guitar Playing* has been most gratifying, in terms both of kindly comment by teachers and of an increasing pattern of private and school adoption since its first appearance in 1968. However with wider use comes, inevitably, wider criticism, and I am grateful that in almost every case this has been constructive, with suggestions for possible improvement in a later edition.

The supplements in this edition are the result of discussions and correspondence with a large number of dedicated classical guitar teachers, and I should like to acknowledge with thanks the time that they have taken to explain their experience in the practical usage of the book.

I agreed with them in finding the transition from single line melodies to music in more than one part too abrupt; and the relevant sections have been considerably enlarged with a new chapter on chords.

For class use, as well as for amateurs who like to play together, an appendix of easy music in three and four parts has been added. I have found these immensely helpful myself in the encouragement of sight reading and in the development of musical taste through uncomplicated experience with better composers. Also, didactic purposes apart, they seem to be a source of great enjoyment to the participants.

The section on daily exercises has been rewritten and enlarged, and many practical exercises for the right hand have been added to the earlier lessons.

Of course sheer limitations of space make it impossible to put in everything that would ideally be included. It has become necessary to call a halt and to leave to the next volume the task of filling in such musical and technical gaps as may be present in this work. The paramount task of a first book is, in my view, to instill a taste for the subject and the desire to continue more deeply into it. My sincere hope is that this new edition will continue to do just that.

Preface to the First Edition

My first book, *Playing the Guitar,* was designed to whet the appetite of the person who had found an interest in the guitar by illustrating various styles. This present volume is for the person who wishes to express him- or herself through the beautiful voice of the solo guitar.

The guitar has a magnetic attraction for those who have heard its tone and range of sensitivity demonstrated. Whether the seed was sown by the sound of Segovia or some other great player, my object here is to initiate the reader into the mystery, or apparent one, of this most eloquent of instruments.

In fairness to the majority I have started at the beginning and expected no prior knowledge, and if the reader can discover even a part of the pleasure that I have had from my years of association with the guitar, then my purpose has been achieved.

I should like to express thanks to my good friend Howard Heitmeyer for consistent help and encouragement in the preparation of this work. I should also like to thank Abraham Chelst for help in discovering sources of repertoire material and for making available to me his careful translations of the tablature of Gaspar Sanz into modern notation.

Introduction

The guitar today is enjoying a level of popularity unprecedented in history, and it is giving competition even to the piano as the household instrument of the musical family. While many use the instrument only as an accompaniment to the voice, more and more people are seeking to develop their abilities and explore the solo potential of the guitar, to the extent that few major cities do not now have at least one guitar society where amateurs may meet and perform.

Perhaps the closest historical parallel is afforded by the English Elizabethan period, when the guitar's companion instrument, the lute, achieved a leading position among both professionals and amateurs. The situation was similar in the other European countries except Spain, where the preferred instrument was the vihuela, strung like the lute, but somewhat more like a guitar in shape. Both instruments owe their introduction into Europe to the Moorish invasion of Spain in 711.

The seventeenth century saw a sharp decline of interest in the lute, probably because of the extra strings now added to it, increasing its complexity and the difficulties of tuning. However, at the end of the century a new craze took over, this time for the guitar. At this time the guitar was strung with five pairs of strings, comparable to the upper five strings of the modern guitar. Such was its popularity at the court of Charles II that the scene there was described by a contemporary as one of "universal strumming," and much the same situation existed in the French court of Louis XIV, who was also a player.

The composers for the guitar of this period were mostly performers themselves, as was the case with the lute. Among the most popular were Francisco Corbetta, Robert de Visée, and Gaspar Sanz, whose music exhibits accomplishment and charm but lacks the sophistication of the great lutenists, such as Dowland, Holborne, Rosseter, Cutting, and many others.

After enjoying a period in the favor of fashionable society, the guitar faced a decline in popularity in the mid-eighteenth century attributed at least partially to the determined efforts of one man. Jacob Kirkman, a harpsichord maker, devised the plan of making the guitar unfashionable by presenting large quantities of cheap instruments to servant girls, street musicians, and the like. It seems he was successful, since the harpsichord soon returned to favor. In 1815 a revival of enthusiasm for the guitar in England was heralded by the arrival in London of the Spanish virtuoso-composer Fernando Sor. The instrument had now acquired a sixth string, enhancing its range and musical capabilities, which were very ably demonstrated by Sor in both his compositions and his performances. Yet in spite of the success of Sor and his able contemporaries Aguado and Giuliani, the tide of popularity of the guitar again turned, and Sor died in comparative obscurity in 1839.

It was again a Spaniard who revived public interest in the guitar as a solo instrument. Francisco Tárrega (1852–1909) is rightfully credited with being the founder of the modern school of guitarists. His remarkable playing, his innovations of technique, and his many compositions and transcriptions laid a firm foundation for the present-day position of respect and dignity occupied by the concert guitar. Through him composers and players came to realize that the capabilities of the instrument extended far beyond the secondary role of accompaniment. Isaac Albeniz, after hearing

Tárrega play some of his compositions that Tárrega had transcribed for the guitar, declared that he preferred them to his piano originals.

Tárrega's work was continued by his pupils, notably Miguel Llobet and Emilio Pujol, and added to by the remarkable genius of the guitarist who became a legend in his own time, Andrés Segovia. Thanks to the untiring work of this virtuoso, the guitar now attracts audiences in concert halls all over the world, and performers and composers favor the instrument as never before in history.

How to Use This Book

If you are beginning the formal study of the guitar with a teacher, you will have no particular problem, since your teacher will allocate lessons and exercises at a time appropriate to your stage of learning and will, if necessary, refer you back to a former lesson when he or she believes that points have been overlooked or insufficiently absorbed. If, however, you have decided to teach yourself, with no more assistance than this book and your enthusiasm, then the following points will be important to you if you are successfully to fulfill the functions of both teacher and pupil.

First, and most important, do not try to go too fast. The fact that you can *read* to advanced lessons quickly does not mean that you are ready for the lesson, and skipping to more advanced work before laying the necessary foundation is likely to make you feel frustrated and lacking in ability. There are at least two years of study contained in these pages, so do not be afraid to take your time and repeat exercises or studies until you, in your capacity as teacher, believe that they have been satisfactorily mastered.

Second, give the most scrupulous attention to the sections and illustrations on hand positions. Usually, much of a teacher's time during the first few months is spent correcting faulty hand positions, and this is the point at which you are most likely to go wrong when instructing yourself. The positions are unfamiliar at first, but they are designed, after many centuries of experience, to give you the maximum dexterity and facility. Early exercises and pieces *can* be played with faulty positions, but trouble arises when more ambitious pieces are approached, at which time it is far harder to correct the faults that have become habits.

At each stage of the book have your guitar in hand, ready to play, so that examples and illustrations given in the text can be tried out in context. The book has been designed essentially as a *practical* course of study, and by *doing* you will learn.

SUGGESTED STUDY PLAN

First, be prepared to give up to four weeks to any lesson. The stages will include experimentation, frustration, practice, and finally achievement. Where possible, try to find someone to accompany the exercises, or play along with the audio cassettes. You will find that they sound completely different with the accompaniments and can be the source of much enjoyment and fun while learning.

Second, set aside a certain time for playing each day and try to be consistent. As with physical exercises, you will achieve far more by doing some study every day than by occasional, if strenuous, exertion.

Finally, remember that the teacher can say things over and over again, whereas the author can usually say them only once. This places a great burden on you to be conscientious in your reading and to reread the important sections several times. Self-teaching can be amazingly effective, but the burden is on you to be as scrupulous a teacher as you are a pupil.

A Note to the Teacher

Almost all the exercises in this book have been designed as duets. The reason for this is that the exercises, as opposed to the studies and performance pieces, have a single didactic purpose; and in most cases this purpose is best recognized and accomplished with a single melodic line, uncluttered with difficult harmony or other sight-reading problems. The harmonic function is thus left to the teacher or, where there is none, to a friend at a more advanced stage. My experience has been that this duet approach does much to take the dryness out of, for instance, a ligado exercise or the learning of the notes of a new position, and it is my hope that other teachers will find this method effective and enjoyable.

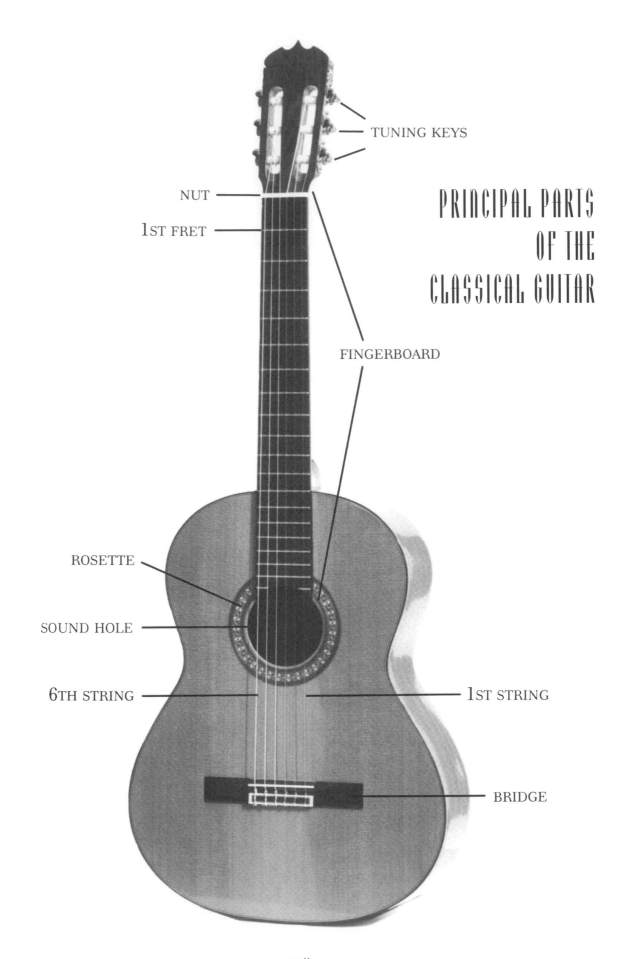

TUNING KEYS

NUT

1ST FRET

PRINCIPAL PARTS
OF THE
CLASSICAL GUITAR

FINGERBOARD

ROSETTE

SOUND HOLE

6TH STRING

1ST STRING

BRIDGE

COMPLETE NOTES OF THE GUITAR

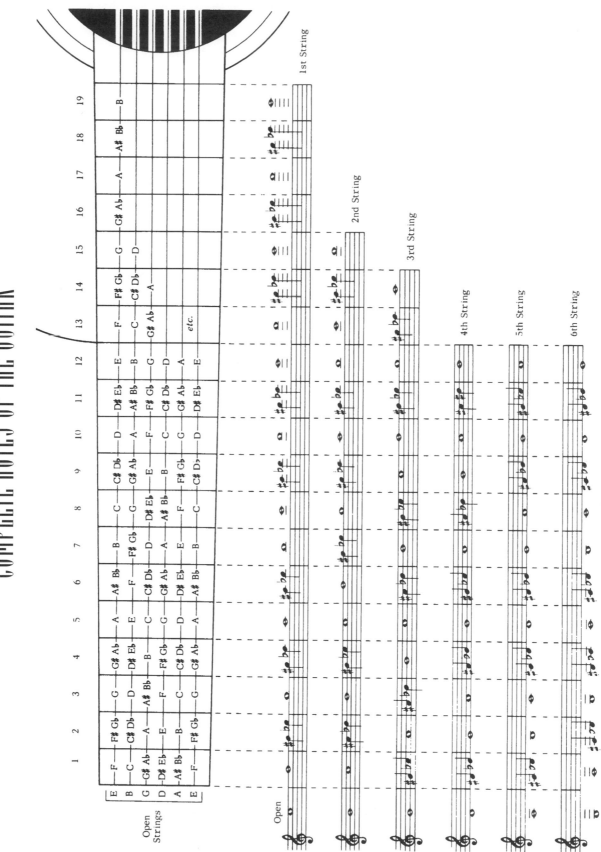

Solo Guitar Playing

CLASSICAL POSITION

Basic Technique

The following two lessons are perhaps the most important in this book, since they cover all the basic movements normally used for playing solos. It is important to observe the playing position closely and to try to form good habits from the very beginning.

PLAYING POSITION

If you study the illustrations of the classical position, you will notice that the left foot is raised and resting on a small footstool. A popular and readily available type of footstool can be adjusted in height to suit the individual and also folded flat for traveling or storage. This enables the upper part of the left leg to provide a stable resting place for the guitar. The guitar touches the chest but is not held in tightly since the back of the guitar also needs to resonate. Note that the right forearm rests at the widest part of the instrument. The left hand is free to move and is not supporting the weight of the guitar.

An alternative to using the footstool is to use a cushion or similar device on the left upper leg, which supports the guitar and raises it slightly. Sitting this way both feet remain flat on the floor, which some consider advantageous to the back. Various devices are sold for this purpose. In essence the guitar is in the same position whichever method is used, and the instructions for the position and usage of the right and left hands are the same for either. When you take up the position, note particularly the following points:

1. You should sit on the front of the chair, holding the guitar upright and leaning forward slightly.

To see your hands, bend the head forward, rather than pulling the guitar back.

2. The weight of your right arm is taken on the guitar–do not let the elbow project over the edge, as this alters the angle of your right hand.

3. The right hand should be able to hang loosely, with the knuckles along the same line as the strings.

4. Your wrist must *not* touch the face of the guitar–when you play it will be raised about 3½ inches.

CLASSICAL POSITION, FROM THE RIGHT

1

TUNING

The first step now, of course, is to tune the guitar, and this presents something of a problem to the beginner. Do not be discouraged if your first attempts are not quite accurate–ease of tuning *does* come with practice.

If you tune to a piano, consult the sketch shown here to locate the notes for each of the six strings.

Alternatively, you can use a pitch pipe, which can be obtained with six separate pipes, each giving the tone for one of the guitar strings. Probably the most accurate pitch is given by a tuning fork. The way to use this is as follows: Hold the fork by the stem and give one of the prongs a sharp tap on your knee. While it is still vibrating, press the base of the stem on the face of your guitar so that the fork is vertical, in relation to the guitar, with the prongs uppermost. The vibration is thus transferred to the wood of the guitar, resulting in a clear tone.

CLASSICAL POSITION, FROM THE LEFT

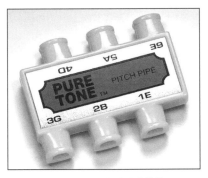

GUITAR PITCH PIPE

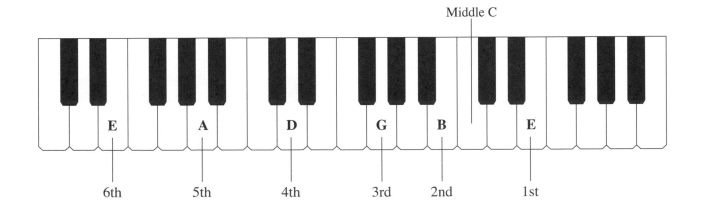

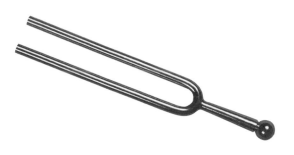

TUNING FORK

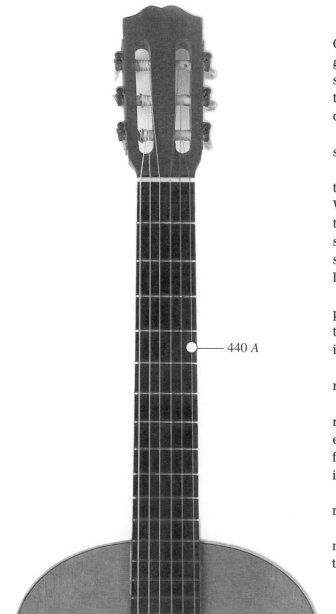

440 A

However, it is important to note that most tuning forks give the note *A* at 440 cycles. This note is produced on the guitar at the 5th fret of the 1st string.

Since this entails continually finding the note each time you adjust the string, it is less convenient at this point than the other methods. If it is possible to find a fork tuned to the *E* given by the first string, open (i.e., without any fret stopped), then this may be used without difficulty and will be more accurate than a pitch pipe.

RELATIVE TUNING

Of course it is most important that the strings of the guitar be tuned in correct relation to each other. A slight error in pitch is not too important as long as the guitar is in tune with itself, and this may be done as follows:

1. Tune the 6th (lowest) string as close as possible by any of the above methods.

2. Put a left hand finger behind the 5th fret of this string and sound the note with the right hand. We have now produced a *reference note* for tuning the *5th string*. Adjust the tuning key for the 5th string until the note of the open 5th string is the same as the note produced at the 5th fret of the lowest (6th) string.

3. When the 5th string is in tune, repeat the procedure by placing a finger behind the 5th fret of the *5th string*. This gives the reference note for tuning the 4th string.

4. Again, the 5th fret of the 4th string gives the reference note for tuning the 3rd string.

5. With the 3rd string in tune, we now require a reference note to tune the 2nd string. This is the exception. The reference note is found by putting a finger behind the *4th* fret of the 3rd string, and tuning the 2nd string to this.

6. Finally, the 5th fret of the 2nd string gives the reference note for tuning the 1st string.

This method sounds complicated at first, but is not at all difficult once you have done it a few times.

ELECTRONIC TUNERS

Much of the difficulty of tuning can be avoided by using one of the electronic tuners now available. The tuners "listen" when you play a note and indicate what the note is (*A, B, C*, etc.) and whether it is above, below, or precisely at the correct pitch for that note. The indicator may be a needle pointer that swings to either side of a center point or individual indicator lights for above, below, or on pitch.

The advantage of such a device is that any guesswork is eliminated since the process is automatic and usually very accurate. However, such precision instruments are predictably quite expensive compared to the other tuning aids.

BEGINNING TO PLAY

The Rest Stroke

This stroke is the most fundamental and useful in playing successions of single notes on the guitar. It is also the means of developing a strong clear tone with the right hand, and probably the greatest difference between the professional and the amateur player lies in the use and handling of the rest stroke.

The movement should at first be divided into two stages.

1. *Preparation:* The very tip of the finger touches the string to be played, so that the string is adjacent to the nail.

2. *Completion:* The finger presses down and across to rest on the next string. In the process the nail catches the original string and sets it vibrating. For the best tone this vibration should be in a plane vertical to the face of the guitar.

The essence of this stroke is that the finger does not pluck out from the guitar, but presses down and comes to rest on the next string. Notice particularly that at the completion of the stroke, the finger is curved in the same way it was at the beginning and has not straightened out. Allowing the finger to straighten takes power from the stroke and can lead to a weak touch. Of particular importance is the angle of the finger in relation to the string. This is illustrated by the photographs on page 5 and the drawings on page 12. Note that the finger is not vertical to the string, but angled slightly so that the stroke is made with the left side of the nail as you look down on it.

The more the angle, the less the nail will catch; thus for greatest attack and volume the finger will be more vertical, but for a softer tone it will be angled more. The nail itself should be shaped in an even curve following the contour of the fingertip, with no corners at the side that might catch unevenly on the string.

The quality of sound depends upon the smoothness of the nail surface. After filing, the nails should be polished on the surfaces that strike the string with a very fine (600 grade) sandpaper.

Be prepared to experiment at length with this stroke until a clear fullbodied tone can be produced. The tendency of the last joint of the finger to straighten in completing the stroke can be corrected more easily as the correct muscles are developed; but from the start care should be taken to avoid this bad habit. It can be hard to correct later.

In addition to the basic stroke, experiment with sliding the nail at a slight angle across the string in the direction of the bridge for a more delicate sound.

Alternation

An important early rule to remember is that successive notes are not played by the same finger of the right hand but are produced by alternating fingers, usually the index and middle.

To play four successive notes on the open 1st string, follow this procedure:

1. Execute a rest stroke with the index finger as described earlier. After completion of the stroke, the fingers should be resting on the 2nd string.

2. Bring the middle finger down to the preparation position on the 1st string. Then, as you play the note with the middle finger, raise the index finger

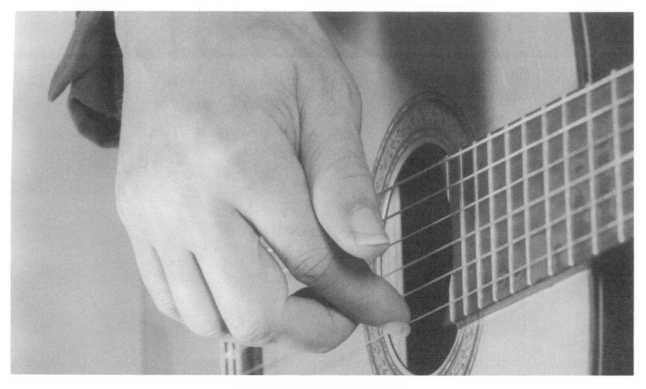

REST STROKE (PREPARATION)

REST STROKE (COMPLETION)

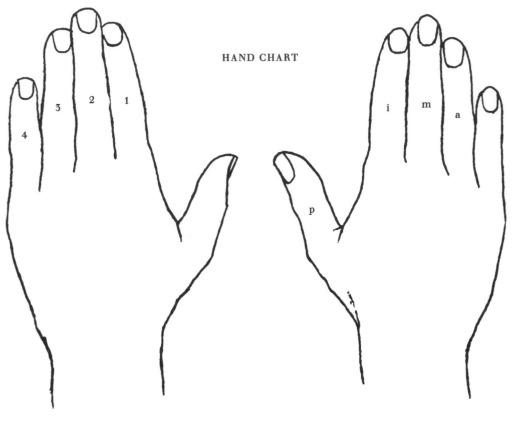

HAND CHART

LEFT HAND   RIGHT HAND

clear of the strings. The middle finger is now rest-ing on the 2nd string.

3. Bring the index finger to the preparation po-sition on the 1st string. Complete the stroke, raising the middle finger as you do so.

4. Conclude by playing a rest stroke with the middle finger, raising the index finger as you do so. From a side view the two fingers alternating give the impression of two legs walking, or more accu-rately climbing, a shallow flight of stairs. Like walking, alternation is a "feel" that once acquired, becomes completely automatic.

Naming the Fingers

By tradition the fingers of the right hand are known by the initial letters of the Spanish words for them:

p	for *pulgar*	Thumb
i	for *indicio*	Index finger
m	for *medio*	Middle finger
a	for *anular*	Ring finger

The little finger of the right hand is not used.

The left hand fingers are numbered from one to four starting with the index. Note that this is *not* the same as the piano numbering. A zero sign beside a note indicates no left hand finger, that is, that the string is sounded open.

THE LEFT HAND

As a first exercise for the left hand, try the follow-ing movements, which will strengthen and in-crease the stretch of your fingers:

LEFT HAND POSITION

1. With the hand in position as above, bring the 1st finger firmly down just behind the 1st fret of the 6th (thickest) string, making the loudest sound possible.

2. *Without lifting the 1st finger,* hammer the 2nd finger down behind the 2nd fret of the same string.

3. Repeat the procedure with the 3rd and 4th fingers. Remember to leave each finger on when it has hammered.

4. Move to the 5th string and repeat the movements. Continue up each string in succession.

The most important points in establishing the left hand position are as follows:

RELAXED ARM AND WRIST. Do not let the elbow stick out—try to relax the whole arm from shoulder to wrist.

THUMB BEHIND THE NECK. Do not let the thumb creep round from the back of the neck—this cramps the left hand and reduces the distance your fingers can reach.

VERTICAL FINGERS. When hammering, each finger should come down vertically on its extreme tip. At first you will find this difficult with the 4th finger, but practice will quickly remedy this.

PREPARATION FOR THE NEXT LESSON

Before approaching lesson two, practice the following:

1. Alternate rest strokes on the first three strings. Play four notes on each string evenly and clearly, starting sometimes with the index, sometimes with the middle finger, and observe strict alternation.

2. Give plenty of practice to the left hand exercise just described. You can *hear* your improvement as the fingers gain strength and accuracy.

3. Check your position carefully each time you sit down to play. If necessary use a mirror and compare your position with that in the photographs.

4. Go slowly. It is much more important to be accurate and methodical than to try for speed at this point.

Right Hand Techniques

After practicing the rest stroke, which is the principal technique for playing single melodic lines, it is time to learn the correct method for playing chords and broken chords (arpeggios).

CHORDS

But chords and arpeggios start with the same movement–a preparatory placement of the thumb and fingers of the right hand so as to select the strings to be played.

The fingers should be on their tips and close to the nails. To complete the movement, the thumb moves forward, and the fingers come back in a contrary or squeezing motion to sound the chord.

These are the points to watch:

1. The right hand does not need to lift from the guitar. In fact the whole movement can be completed without any upward movement of the knuckles.

2. When correctly played, the chord should have a single, harmonic sound, not a ragged succession of notes.

To practice the movement, select the 6th, 3rd, 2nd, and 1st strings. This will give a consonant chord on the open strings.

ARPEGGIOS

As stated before, arpeggios begin the same way chords do, with a right hand placement to select the correct strings. However, in an arpeggio the strings are played one by one, instead of together.

CHORD PREPARATION

CHORD COMPLETION

First, study the photographs carefully. Then try the movement as described next.

1. Place the thumb on the 6th string, fingers on the 3rd, 2nd, and 1st.

2. Play the 6th string so that the thumb comes to rest on the 5th string. Leave it there.

3. Without moving the other fingers, *take out* the index finger to sound the 3rd string. This is a *free stroke.*

4. Without moving the ring finger, repeat the procedure with the middle finger.

5. Finally sound the 1st string with the ring finger. The finger does *not* come to rest but lifts slightly from the guitar.

Note that this is only one form of arpeggio. The strings may in fact be sounded in any order, and after practicing the above form thoroughly, try some of the following combinations.

1. 6 3 2 1 2 3–6 3 2 1 2 3, etc.
2. 6 3 2 3 1 3 2 3–6 3 2 3 1 3 2 3, etc.
3. 6 1 2 3–6 1 2 3, etc.

In each example use the thumb for the 6th string, index for the 3rd, middle for the 2nd, and ring finger for the 1st.

RULES OF PLACEMENT

For an ascending arpeggio (i.e., 6 3 2 1) place the thumb and all fingers in advance.

For a descending arpeggio (i.e., 6 1 2 3) only the thumb and the next finger to play, in this case the ring finger, need to be placed in advance.

For a combined arpeggio (i.e., 6 3 2 3 1 3 2 3) place the first ascending part of the arpeggio in ad-

vance, in this case the thumb, index, and middle fingers.

The completion of the arpeggio movement has in fact comprised two new techniques. The thumb executed a rest stroke, and the fingers, free strokes.

IDENTIFICATION OF STROKES

Rest Stroke (Thumb)

The rest stroke with the thumb is used when particular emphasis is required in the bass. It is also useful (as indicated earlier) to support the hand in a slow arpeggio. Be sure not to drive the hand forward in playing the thumb rest stroke. Simply let the weight of the thumb fall to the next string.

Free Stroke (Thumb)

In fast-moving arpeggios it is not necessary to rest the thumb when this might inhibit speed. In this case the thumb moves forward, after playing the note, to a position slightly above the strings (free stroke). This is in fact the most usual stroke for the thumb. Note particularly that the joint of the thumb does not bend in either the rest or free stroke.

Free Stroke (Fingers)

In addition to the arpeggio the free stroke is used for tonal contrast with the rest stroke, or when a rest stroke would damp the adjacent string when this string is meant to continue sounding. This will become clear in the practical work of later lessons.

As far as possible the free stroke, as well as the rest stroke, should set the string in motion in a

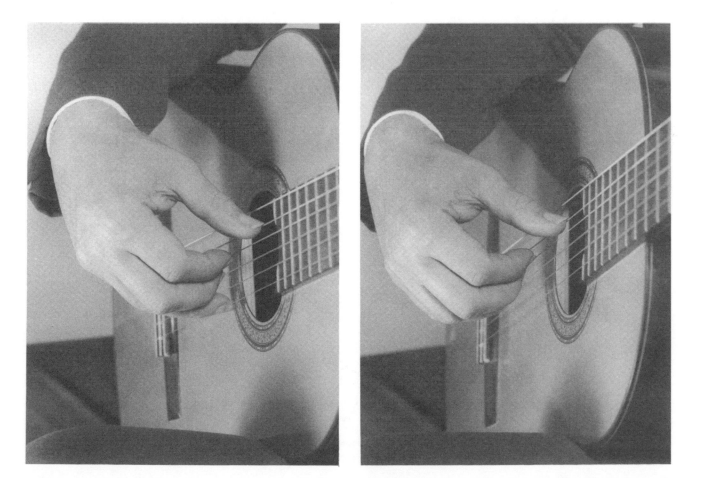

plane perpendicular to the face of the guitar, as in the accompanying diagrams, and not parallel to it. However, the vertical component of the movement is caused by the initial placement of the finger on the string; this presses it down slightly. After re-

leasing the string, the finger completes the more lateral movement, as shown.

Before approaching the next lesson, practice all the movements described so far, and check your-self with the self-test that follows.

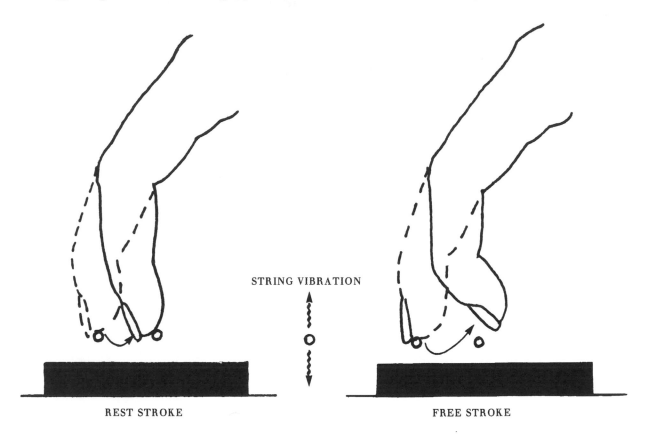

STRING VIBRATION

REST STROKE   FREE STROKE

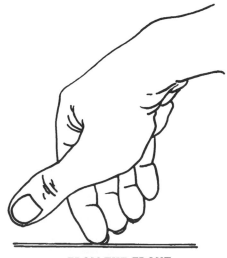

FROM THE FRONT

TEST NUMBER ONE

1. Where is the nut of the guitar located?

2. In relative tuning, which fret on the 3rd string gives the reference note for tuning the 2nd string?

3. When the right hand is in correct position to play, what is the direction of the line of the knuckles?

4. Why is alternation used?

5. What is the main use of the rest stroke with the fingers? The thumb?

6. Where should the left hand thumb be located while playing?

7. What is an arpeggio?

8. In what plane should the strings of the guitar vibrate?

9. What part of the fingers actually plays a note?

10. Name and execute the following:

Rest Stroke (Fingers)	Rest Stroke (Thumb)
Alternation	Chord
Free Stroke (Fingers)	Free Stroke (Thumb)
Arpeggio	

Beginning to Read Music

It is hard to overemphasize the importance of training yourself to sight-read well, and the reasons are clear. First, you will be able to study and complete a performance piece in a reasonably short time, particularly before you have lost your initial enthusiasm for it. Second, you will have the additional pleasure of being able to read through anthologies and collections much as you would read a book. Third, you will be able to join other musicians to play duets or ensemble pieces.

Guitarists are notoriously poor readers compared to other instrumentalists. They tend to learn pieces by laboriously working them out measure by measure, attempting to memorize as they go. If you can avoid this trap you will progress much faster in the long run, and become a better all-around musician.

TWO RULES

Perhaps the two most important rules to remember are these:

1. *Learn to count as you read.*
2. *Keep your eyes on the music, and do not look back at your left hand.*

MUSICAL NOTATION

Standard musical notation for both the guitar and other instruments consists of notes drawn on five lines and enclosing four spaces, known as a musical staff. Each line and each space represents one note in the musical spectrum, and the position of the staff in the overall range of musical notes is in-

dicated by a "clef sign," so that the notes on any given staff always come in the middle range of the instrument for which the staffs is usually used.

Clef Sign

Music for the guitar is written in the "treble clef" as indicated by the sign above. The notes of the treble clef are:

They are easily learned by separating the lines from the spaces.

Lines

Spaces

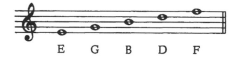

Obviously the staff does not contain enough notes for the full range of the guitar, so additional notes are added by drawing lines above and below the staff. These are known as "ledger lines." The diagram that follows shows the complete range of the guitar, with ledger lines drawn where necessary.

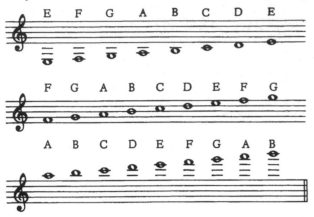

Note that only the letters *A* to *G* are used in naming the notes, and that each letter therefore re-occurs every eighth note. The interval from any note to the next one of the same letter is known as an "octave," and your ear will recognize that notes having the same letter have a similarity, although separated in pitch.

TIME AND COUNTING

The duration of each sound is indicated by the type of note drawn on the line or space. Here are the most common notes:

♩	Quarter note (crochet)	1 count
♪	Half note (minim)	2 counts
♩.	Dotted half note (dotted minim)	3 counts
o	Whole note (semibreve)	4 counts

Notice that the duration is given in counts, not in absolute time (such as 1/10 second, etc.). There is no fixed time period for a given symbol, since we count faster or slower according to an indication (tempo marking) at the beginning of a piece. What is fixed is the *relationship* between the notes, so that whatever the speed of our count, the half note will last twice as long as the quarter note, the whole note four times as long, and so on.

For convenience, music is divided into short sections known as bars or measures, indicated by vertical lines and containing a fixed number of counts. This number is also indicated at the beginning of the line and is known as the "time signature." Here are some examples:

(a)   (b)   (c)

The upper number gives the number of counts in each measure, the lower number the type of note that receives one count. In the first example (a), each measure will receive four counts, each count indicated by one quarter note.

In the second example (b), each measure will contain three counts, each indicated by one quarter note. The third example (c) also gives three counts to each measure, but here each count is worth a half note.

To relate this to the guitar, try playing and counting exercises 1 to 4 on the 1st string open, using alternating rest strokes with the right hand.

Exercise 1

Exercise 2

Exercise 3

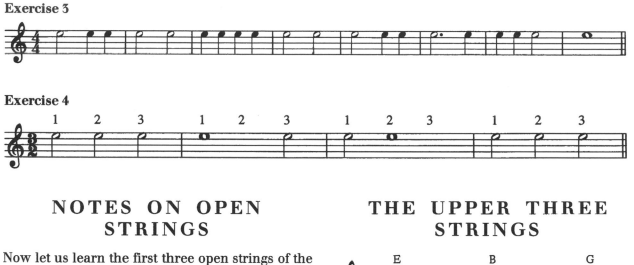

Exercise 4

NOTES ON OPEN STRINGS

THE UPPER THREE STRINGS

Now let us learn the first three open strings of the guitar, and try the exercises in note recognition and counting. Remember particularly to

1. Go slow but keep the count even.
2. Count and play simultaneously.

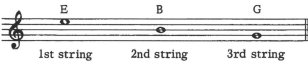

In exercise 5, and in most of the exercises that follow, the lower staff is an accompaniment part for the teacher. It will be found that the exercises sound more interesting musically when played as duets.

Exercise 5

Exercise 6

Exercise 7

THE LOWER THREE STRINGS

Now add the remaining strings, and be sure that *all* the open strings are thoroughly memorized before continuing to the next lesson. Use the thumb on the lower three strings and fingers on the upper three as indicated at the beginning of exercise 8.

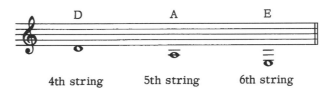

4th string   5th string   6th string

Exercise 8

Exercise 9

Exercise 10

Exercise 11

ARPEGGIO EXERCISES FOR DAILY PRACTICE

Start slowly and increase speed only when each note is clear and even. Each pattern is slightly more difficult than the one before, so practice each one thoroughly before moving on to the next.

Exercise 12

Exercise 13

Exercise 14

Exercise 15

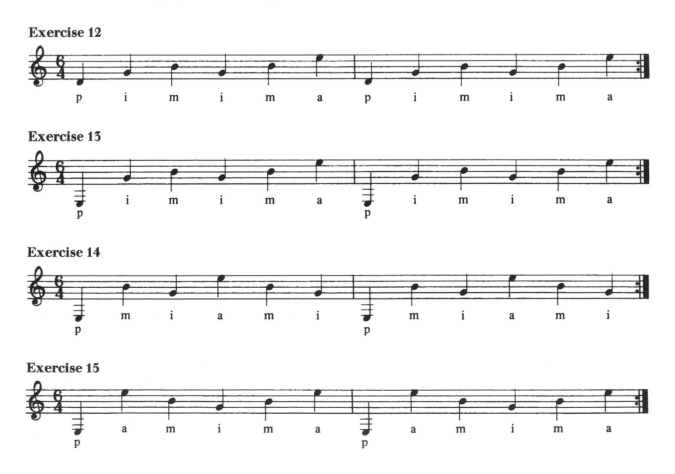

Notes on the Frets

The purpose of the next five lessons is to learn as thoroughly as possible the notes of the first four frets of each string. It is a mistake to try to hurry this stage, and the exercises should be repeated until they can be played without a break in the tempo.

FINGERING

Unless otherwise indicated be careful to use the 1st finger for the 1st fret, 2nd for the 2nd fret, and so on. On the right hand continue to use *rest strokes* with the fingers, free strokes with the thumb.

NOTES ON THE FIRST STRING

After playing these notes over a few times to memorize them, try the following exercises. Care should be taken to play on the extreme tips of the left hand fingers. It is important to form this habit from the beginning. It is equally important to play very close to the frets—it should be possible just to feel the side of the fret with the fingertip.

COMMON TIME AND INCOMPLETE MEASURES

The *C* at the beginning of exercise 16 is an abbreviation for common time or $\frac{4}{4}$.

Exercise 21 begins with an incomplete measure. This is quite common, the convention being that the last (part) measure and the first together total one complete measure. In order to begin with the correct count calculate back from the measure line. In this case the initial count must be "four." To balance this the last measure ends on "three."

Exercise 16

Exercise 17

Exercise 18

Exercise 19

Exercise 20

Exercise 21

An important point of technique is that it is often not necessary to take a left hand finger away when moving to a higher note on the same string, as may be seen by playing this example.

The 1st finger, after playing the *F*, should remain on the string for two reasons:

1. It is easier to put the 3rd finger on the *G* when the 1st finger is in place.

2. The 1st finger is in position for the *F* at the end of the measure without having to move.

As a general rule it is easier to find a note when at least one finger is already on the fingerboard since this finger holds the left hand in position.

NOTES ON THE SECOND STRING

Now learn these notes on the 2nd string, and try the practice exercises that follow.

Note that special care is needed when coming from the 1st string to the *D* on the 2nd string. Although difficult at first, it soon becomes easier with practice.

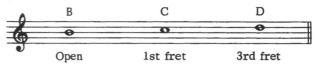

Exercise 22

Exercise 23

Exercise 24

Exercise 25

Exercise 26

Exercise 27

Exercise 28

Exercise 29

Exercise 30

Exercise 31

Exercise 31 (continued)

EXERCISES FOR DAILY
TECHNIQUE PRACTICE

As before, practice slowly with clarity, then increase speed. Note that the thumb is sometimes (though not customarily) used on the 3rd string.

ARPEGGIOS

Exercise 32

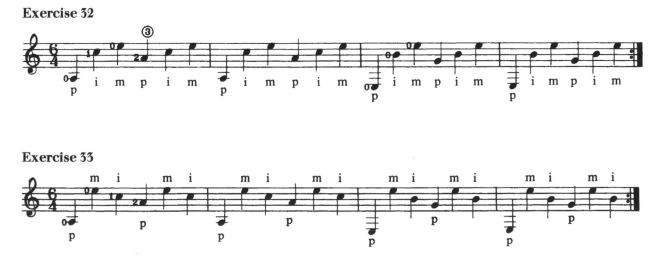

Exercise 33

Exercise 34

ALTERNATION AND SCALES

Exercise 35

Exercise 36

Notes, Rests, and Ties

This lesson adds notes on the 3rd and 4th strings to those already learned. Practice *all* the exercises aiming at producing a clear sound and even timing.

NOTES ON THE THIRD STRING

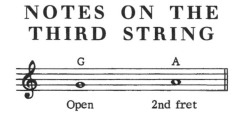

NOTES ON THE FOURTH STRING

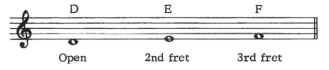

Exercise 37

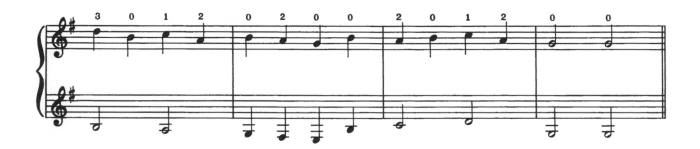

Exercise 38

Exercise 39

RESTS

Each period of silence in music must be as accurately indicated as a note. The silence is known as a rest, and the rests are named like notes of similar time value.

—   Whole note rest   (o)

—   Half note rest   (♩)

𝄽   Quarter note rest   (♩)

TIES

A note may be sustained from one measure to the next by use of the "tie" sign. The first note only should be played, but it is held for the total duration of the two notes.

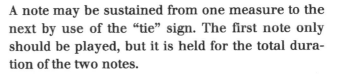

In this example the *F* is played on the count of four and held through the first count of the next measure.

Exercise 40

In the following exercises it is suggested that you count them through first. Then try to count and play simultaneously. In exercise 41 use the arpeggio technique—free strokes with the fingers.

Exercise 41

Exercise 41 (continued)

Exercise 42

Exercise 43

Exercise 44

Exercise 45

Exercise 46

In exercise 47 pay particular attention to the right hand fingering. The ring finger (*a*) is introduced in places where the simple alternation of *i* and *m* would be awkward.

Exercise 47

Exercise 48

ARPEGGIO PRACTICE

Leave the left hand fingers on the strings whenever possible; for example, in the second line in exercise 49 leave the 2nd and 4th fingers in position for the first five measures. When the pattern has become familiar, the right hand may be varied as shown in exercises 49a and 49b.

Exercise 49

Exercise 49a

Exercise 49b

More Advanced Counting

FASTER NOTES

Notes that are faster than quarter notes are drawn by adding one or more tails to the quarter note symbol. Each tail reduces the duration of the note by half.

Equivalent rest

♪ Eighth note

♬ Sixteenth note

♬ Thirty-second note

Succeeding notes of this sort may have the tails joined together thus:

Eighth   Sixteenth   Thirty-second
notes   notes   notes

COUNTING EIGHTH NOTES

Since the eighth note occupies only one-half of one count in common $\frac{4}{4}$ time, it is necessary to "split" the count. The most usual way to do this is to insert an *and* between the number counts.

Quarter notes

Eighth notes

Note that the number counts do not vary in speed, the *ands* are simply inserted between them.

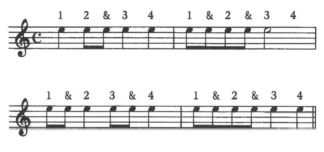

The following exercises should be practiced until they can be played in correct rhythm without pauses. Where necessary the exercises should be counted out loud before playing, and then every effort should be made to count and play simultaneously.

In exercise 51 the incomplete measure starts on a half or *and* beat. The commencing count will be *and four and*. Both exercises 51 and 52 should be studied well as they appear again in lesson eight harmonized in two parts.

Exercise 50

(Folk song)

Exercise 51

Exercise 52

Exercise 52 (continued)

Exercise 53

Exercise 54

TECHNIQUE PRACTICE

Notice in exercise 55 that the ring finger (*a*) is introduced to avoid awkward string crossing. Follow the right hand fingering exactly.

Exercise 55

Remember to place all the fingers on the strings before starting the arpeggio in exercise 56. When the thumb plays, *i, m,* and *a* remain in position. When *i* plays, *m* and *a* remain in position until their turn to play. If this seems unclear, refer to the section on arpeggio practice, page 10.

Exercise 56

For the arpeggio in exercise 57 only the thumb and ring finger (*p* and *a*) are placed in position before starting.

Exercise 57

Notes and Review

This lesson completes the first stage of note learning by adding the 5th and 6th strings. In the next lessons the counting becomes more complex, and sharps and flats are introduced, so it is important before moving on to be very sure of the given notes.

NOTES ON THE FIFTH STRING

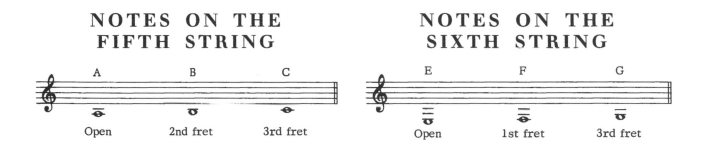

NOTES ON THE SIXTH STRING

Exercise 58

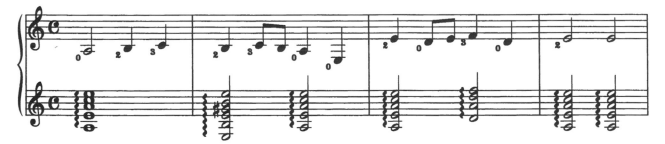

Exercise 59

(Folk Song)

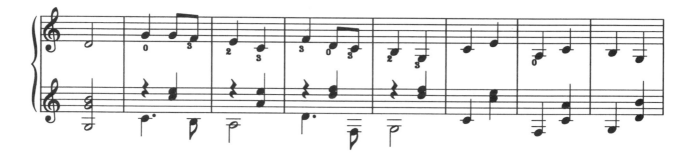

Exercise 60

Moorish Dance

Exercise 61

This a good point to review what you have learned so far. If you have fallen into any of the traps listed here, now is the time to correct them, before they become fixed habits and are hard to unlearn.

TECHNIQUE AND POSITION

When you sit down to play, do you make a conscious effort to assume a correct position? It helps to have a specific place where you practice, with a chair and footstool of the right height and a music stand with the music on it and ready.

Are you keeping your thumb behind the neck of the guitar? If not, you are having unnecessary difficulty in stretching out the fingers.

Are you playing right on the tips of the left hand fingers? If you are, they were probably uncomfortable for a week or two, but this should be wearing off now, and you have formed a correct habit. This becomes more important as more chords are introduced.

When you play with the right hand, does your wrist touch the face of the guitar? Do you rest one of your fingers on the face of the guitar? If the answer is yes to either of these, you are limiting the use of your right hand and should correct the habit before it becomes a serious problem. Remember that for security the thumb may rest on a lower string.

Are you constantly repeating the same finger with the right hand? You probably are, but from now on make a conscious effort to alternate the fingers to increase your speed and ability.

MUSIC READING

Have you made a conscious effort to memorize all the notes so far? Remember that there are many more to come, and you do not want to be held up by having to look back. Particularly be sure of the lower notes on the ledger lines below the staff. These are usually neglected, causing problems when chords are introduced.

Are you watching your left hand when you read music? If so, you are constantly losing your place and, consequently, the continuity of what you are playing. Make a real effort to play by touch when you sight-read—you will be surprised at the result.

Are you finding the notes before you make any effort to count the time? If so your learning is slower than it need be. Remember, count *while* playing, and *before* if this helps.

To complete the notes on the lower strings and for your own recreation, here is a study based on a famous theme by the Spanish composer Albeniz. This is the first real solo, and the study notes should be read carefully, as they are designed to help you through the difficulties.

STUDY NOTES FOR *SPANISH STUDY*

The right hand fingering given in the first measure continues until otherwise indicated. In the same way the left hand fingering is demonstrated only at the beginning and where it is unusual. This makes you read notes rather than fingers, which speeds up your recognition and memorization of the new notes. The melody lies in the bass. The upper *E* is open and does not change, so full attention can be given to the thumb notes.

A   At this point the pattern changes, with three eighth notes occupying the time of one quarter note. This is known as a "triplet," and may be counted *one-and-a two-and-a three-and-a* and so on.

The main counts do not vary, the *one-and-a* occupying the same length of time as the *one-and* in the previous measure.

The 2nd finger remains on the *A* for the rest of the piece. Follow the fingering for the other notes.

Free stroke throughout

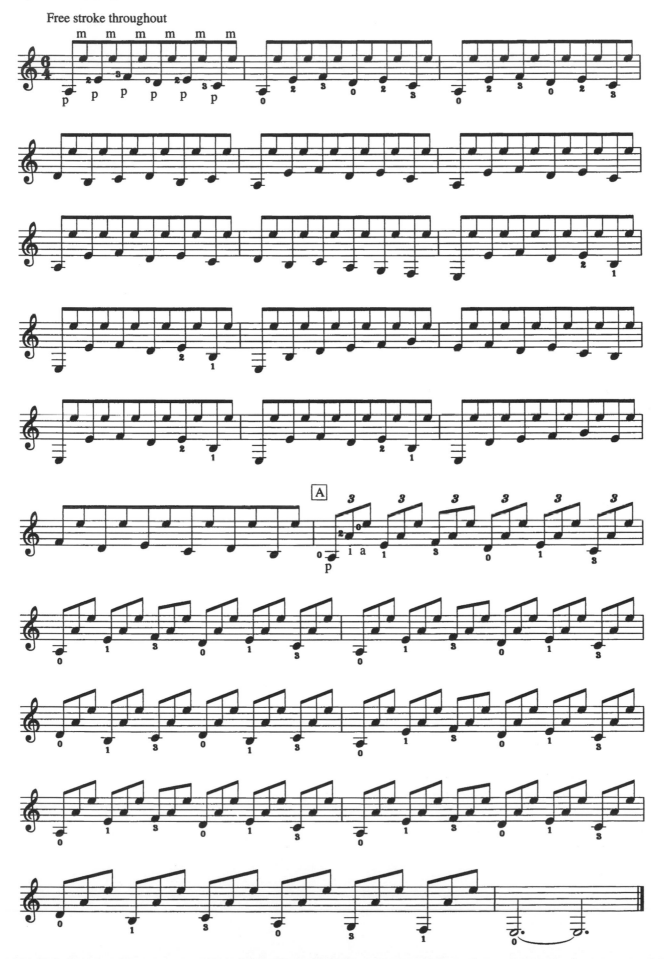

Completion of the First Position

The notes we have learned so far are those of the white keys of the piano. In between lie the black key notes obtained by sharping (raising by a half tone) or flatting (lowering by a half tone) the main notes.

SHARPS AND FLATS

The musical interval from one fret to the next is one half tone. This makes it easy to find any sharp or flat note since it is only necessary to go *up* one fret for the sharp, *down* one fret for the flat. For example, *C* is found at the 1st fret of the 2nd string. *C* sharp (*C♯*) is found at the 2nd fret. Similarly *G* is found at the 3rd fret of the 1st string, *G* flat (*G♭*) at the 2nd fret.

Note that the same fret can be considered as the sharp of the note below or the flat of the note above. The reason for this is considered later in lesson nineteen, under the theory of scales.

Now to add variety to the exercises, here are the complete notes of the first position on the following page.

Note carefully the ways that sharps and flats are indicated in the music.

A sharp or flat sign not only affects the note against which it is drawn, but also every other note of that letter that follows in the same measure. In both the above examples the last note of the measure is *C♯*.

NATURAL SIGNS

To cancel out a sharp or flat sign a *natural* sign must be used (♮).

In both cases the final *C* is natural.

KEY SIGNATURES

When all of a certain note or notes are to be altered in a piece, this is written at the beginning of the line and is known as the *key signature*.

This key signature indicates that *all F*'s and *C*'s must be sharped, whatever octave they are in.

NOTES IN THE FIRST POSITION

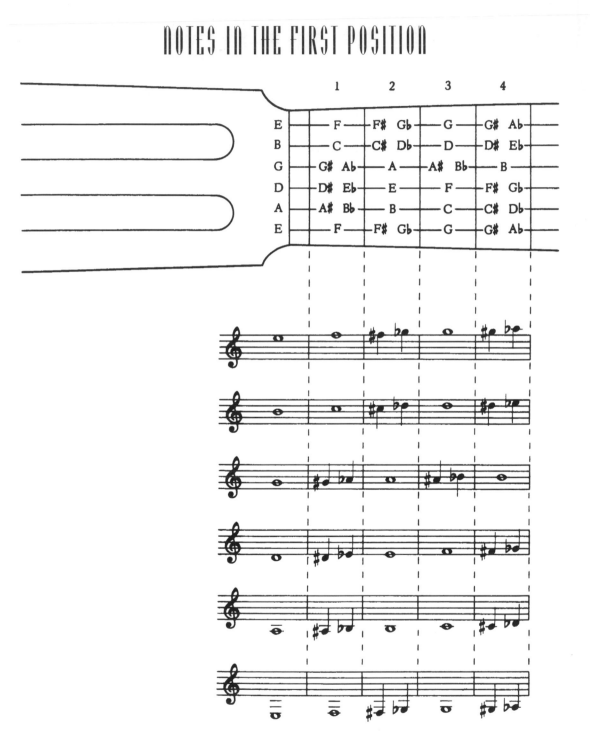

Exercise 62

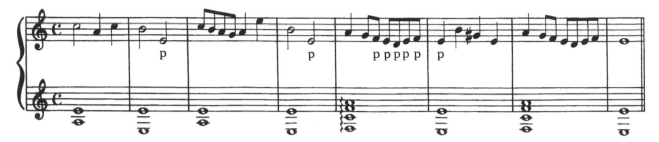

Exercise 63

Exercise 64

Exercise 65

Exercise 66

Exercise 66 (continued)

Exercise 67 gives extra practice in reading the notes of the bottom three strings. The exercise is based on a chorale harmonization by J. S. Bach.

Exercise 67

TECHNIQUE PRACTICE

In exercise 68, practice starting on *i*, then on *m*. Follow the strict alternation throughout.

Exercise 68

Exercise 69

Exercise 70

STUDY NOTES FOR *MALAGUEÑA*

This study is based on a form of song and dance from Malaga. It should be accurate rhythmically, and the final tempo should be fairly brisk.

If you have a metronome, set it to 138 and the click will give you the time for each quarter note. Conventionally this is written ♩ = 138.

In the first measure, place *both* the *E* and the *G♯* with the second and first fingers of the left hand before starting to play. This way it will not be necessary to move the left hand at all for the first two measures. In the third measure leave the second finger on the *A*, so that it is ready for the first note of the fourth measure.

Malagueña

STUDY NOTES FOR
WALTZ AND *ANDANTINO*
by Ferdinando Carulli (1770–1841)

The Neapolitan Ferdinando Carulli was one of the most celebrated guitarists of the early nineteenth century. After moving to Paris he was much in demand as a teacher and published hundreds of compositions in over 330 opus numbers.

Carulli had a particular gift for writing attractive easy pieces, which accounts in part for the tremendous popularity of his teaching method, which is still reprinted today. The *Waltz* and *Andantino* are typical of such pieces and provide good practice for arpeggios and general coordination as well

as recreation. Follow the fingering exactly, particularly where the fourth finger is indicated.

Repeats

The sign ː‖ indicates a repeat from the beginning or from a similar sign pointing the other way ‖ː. The term *D.C.* is an abbreviation of *Da Capo*, meaning "from the beginning." *Al fine* means "to the point marked *fine*" or "end." When playing *Da Capo* it is customary not to make the repeats that occurred on the first playing. In the *Waltz*, this would mean ignoring the repeat sign at the end of the eighth measure.

Waltz   FERDINANDO CARULLI

Waltz (continued)

Andantino   FERDINANDO CARULLI

Introduction to Chords

The basic technique of chords was explained in lesson two, which should be thoroughly reviewed before continuing.

Now that notes of the first position have been learned, it becomes possible to play chords from the music and to practice changing from one to another. Any two notes sounded together form a chord, and the component notes of the chord are written on top of each other, aligned vertically:

When two notes are adjacent it becomes necessary to offset one of them, but all the notes are still sounded simultaneously:

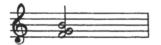

Vocal music is often published with a simplified notation of chords for the guitar. A box is drawn representing part of the fingerboard of the guitar, nut uppermost, and dots show the placement of the left hand fingers:

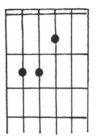

This system is not recommended to the soloist, since it conveys nothing of what the right hand should do. Like all simplified systems it has its drawbacks and is illustrated here only for the purpose of completeness.

The common chords of the guitar will soon become familiar as they recur, and a selection is given in the exercises that follow. Practice sounding the notes exactly together, so that they are heard as a single sound.

Exercise 71

Exercise 71 (continued)

Exercise 72

Exercise 73

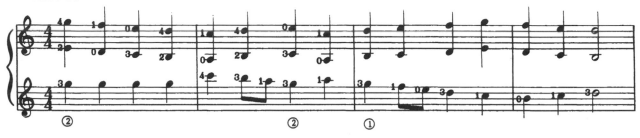

Exercise 74

Exercise 74 (continued)

Exercise 75

Exercise 76

To illustrate the close relationship of chords and arpeggios, exercise 77 follows the same pattern as exercise 76, but with the chords in broken, that is, arpeggio, style. It is a good idea to become very familiar with exercise 76 first, so that you may concentrate on the right hand and the timing.

Exercise 77

Music in Two Lines

Now that you have learned the main principles of reading and have practiced them on single melodic lines, chords, and arpeggios, it is time to approach music in more than one part in which the lines move independently. In practicing the chords in lesson nine, a start was made on playing music in more than one part, but in that lesson each note of the chords had the same duration. In the following sections it will be seen how it is possible to combine melody and harmony to form a complete piece of music.

THE CONCEPT OF VOICES

Historically the development of polyphonic (multi-line) music is closely associated with vocal music, and even today the different lines are often referred to as "voices" although the music is to be played on one or more instruments.

The concept of voices helps to explain why each line must be fully accounted for even though silent: That is to say, the sum of notes and rests must equal the time-value of the measure for each voice.

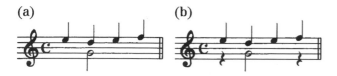

Example (a) is incorrectly written. The lower voice is unaccounted for during two of the four beats. Example (b) is correct, showing with rests that the second line or voice enters after one silent beat and is silent for the final beat of the measure.

COUNTING TWO LINES

Counting more than one line of music should not present undue difficulty, provided that care is taken to see on which beat of the measure each note is to fall. Consider the following example:

The trap *not* to fall into is counting three beats on the first *G* before playing the *F*. Here is the way to consider it:

1. The *G* starts the measure and therefore must fall on the first beat.

2. The upper voice has a rest for one beat only, therefore must enter on the second beat. The *G* must continue sounding since it lasts for three counts.

3. The high *G* falls on the third beat, with the low *G* still sounding.

4. The chord formed by *F* and *G* falls on the fourth beat.

MINIMUM MOVEMENT PRINCIPLE

Now try these exercises in two lines. Remember the technique for chords—free stroke with thumb and fingers. In changing from one chord to another with the left hand, always take the shortest path for the fingers. This is the *minimum movement principle.* It is a basic part of left hand technique.

Notice that there are certain changes in fingering as chords are introduced. The left hand frequently uses the 4th finger at the third fret where this is more comfortable, while the right hand frequently repeats the same finger on successive chords instead of alternating as with single notes.

Naturally it is more difficult to read two lines than one, and at this point accuracy is more important than speed.

Exercise 78

Exercise 79

Exercise 80

Exercise 81

Exercise 82

Exercise 83

Allegro

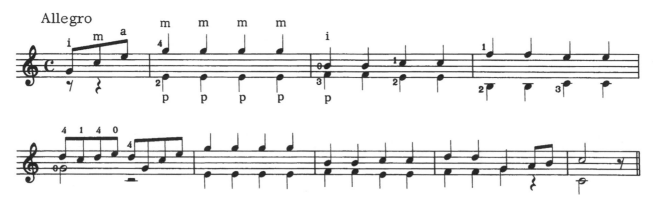

Exercise 84

Exercise 85

Moderato

Ligado Techniques

Smoothness and continuity in playing can be improved by use of a technique known as the *ligado* or *slur*. Different rules apply, according to whether the music is going up or down in pitch; so let us consider separately the ascending and descending ligado.

ASCENDING LIGADO

Two or more notes may be joined by the ligado sign, a curved line, which in the music looks like this:

Here is the procedure for playing this ligado:

1. Play the *B* in the normal way.

2. Hammer down the 1st finger of the left hand to play the *C*. The right hand does not play.

The effect is to join the sound of the two notes in a closer way than can be done when each is played by the right hand. (In Spanish, *ligar* means "to bind.")

Now consider these examples.

Example (a) follows the same rule, except that the first note is not an open string, so the first finger must be in position. The right hand plays the *C*, then the 3rd finger of the left hand hammers down to sound the *D*.

In example (b) the right hand plays the open *B*, then both the *C* and the *D* are hammered by the 1st and 3rd fingers respectively.

Always hammer so that the finger comes down on its *extreme tip* vertically to the fingerboard.

Exercise 86

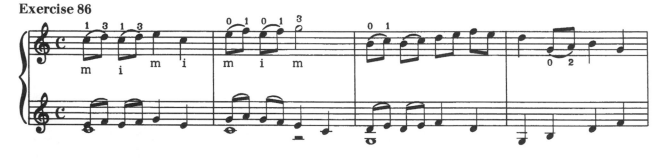

DESCENDING LIGADO

The descending ligado is written musically in exactly the same way.

(a)   (b)

For (a) the procedure is as follows:

1. Play the *C* in the normal way. Leave the left hand 1st finger on the string.

2. With the left hand 1st finger pull sideways off the string to sound the open *B*.

To execute (b):

1. Place both the 3rd and 1st fingers of the left hand in position on the *D* and *C* respectively.

2. Play the *D* in the normal way.

3. Pull the 3rd finger sideways so that it plucks the string and sounds the *C*.

Note particularly that the 1st finger must remain firmly in position throughout, anchoring the string so that it is not pulled out of place by the 3rd finger when it plucks.

The descending ligado requires repeated practice at first. The left hand finger that plucks should start on its extreme tip, so that the pull-off motion can be achieved without great effort. The pressure should be concentrated on the lower finger, which is anchoring the string.

When more than two notes are joined by the ligado sign, the first is played by the right hand, all remaining notes by the left hand using the technique described earlier.

Now try these exercises very slowly and methodically.

Exercise 87

Exercise 88

Exercise 89

Exercise 90

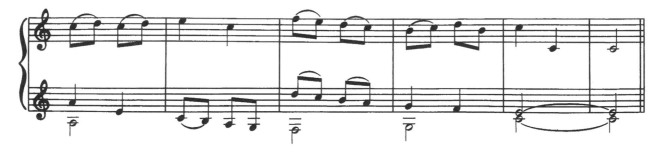

Exercise 91

(Jesu Joy of Man's Desiring)

Exercise 91 (continued)

PATTERNS FOR DAILY PRACTICE

Exercise 92

Exercise 93

Dotted Notes

To be able to learn more interesting and varied solos, it is necessary to learn to count more complex time. One of the main hurdles to be crossed at this point is the counting of dotted notes, and the section that follows should be studied very thoroughly before proceeding to the exercises.

COUNTING DOTTED NOTES

A dot after any note increases the time of that note by half again. When the count is in quarter notes (i.e., $\frac{3}{4}$, $\frac{4}{4}$), it has already been seen that the half note lasts for two counts, the dotted half note for three counts, representing an increase of half the value of the half note, that is, one count.

The Dotted Quarter Note

The dotted quarter note follows the same rule and lasts for one count plus one half count. Perhaps the easiest way to see this is to compare the dotted quarter note with an equivalent number of eighth notes, since we have already learned that they occupy a half count.

Both lines occupy the same length of time, one and a half counts. The eighth notes would be counted *one and two,* and so the dotted quarter note should be sustained for the same count.

In the time signatures under consideration, the dotted quarter note is usually followed by an eighth note, giving a characteristic lilt to the rhythm. This can be seen by playing and counting the familiar tune *Greensleeves.*

When you are experienced in counting the dotted quarter note, the *and* between the *one and two* may be omitted.

Exercise 94

Exercise 95

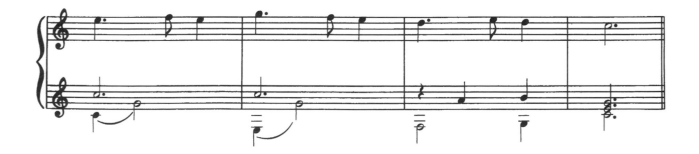

Exercise 96

(Folk song)

Exercise 97

(Theme by Vivaldi)

TEST NUMBER TWO

1. **Find these notes on the guitar**

   On the 1st string *F*♯

   On the 2nd string *D*

   On the 3rd string *B*

   On the 4th string *F*

   On the 5th string *C*♯

   On the 6th string *G*♯

2. **Mark the notes from question 1 on the staff provided.**

3. **Explain how in $\frac{4}{4}$ time a note may be written to last five counts.**

4. **What is the symbol for an eighth note rest?**

5. **What is the musical interval from one fret to the next?**

6. **How is the ligado indicated in music?**

7. **What are the rules for the descending ligado?**

8. **What is the minimum movement principle?**

9. **Write under the staff where each beat of the measure falls in the following example:**

10. **Play the example in question 9 in correct time.**

11. **Explain the rules of the arpeggio technique.**

12. **Play the daily technique exercises you have memorized.**

FIVE PIECES WITH STUDY NOTES

GREENSLEEVES
Anonymous

The principal technical purpose of this piece is to improve your ability to handle two-note chords. Practice first for completely simultaneous sounding of the two notes. Later, when the piece is familiar, you may experiment with a rest stroke on the upper note to bring out the melody. This is facilitated by sounding the lower note a fraction before the upper one, producing a slight arpeggiation of the chord. This should not be overdone, and in this piece would be the most satisfactory on the first beat of the measure, which carries a slight accent.

A At this point the 2nd finger has to jump from the 3rd to the 4th string. Practice this movement until a smooth transition can be made.

B In this measure the 4th finger should reach out for the *F*♯ without any change of position of the thumb and hand. To ensure this, leave the 1st finger on the *G*♯ throughout the measure.

Greensleeves

ETUDE
by Ferdinando Carulli (1770–1841)

This piece affords a good opportunity to practice the upward four-note arpeggio. Aim for an even, flowing tempo, with an eventual metronome speed of about ♩ = 96.

A   At this point place both the 1st and 2nd fingers of the left hand. With the right hand place *p*, *i*, *m*, and *a* in preparation for the arpeggio movement.

B   Place 2nd and 4th fingers simultaneously to prepare the *B* and *D*.

C   Finding the *D*♯ accurately with the 4th finger presents the main difficulty of this piece. Keep the finger as vertical as possible to avoid touching the open *E* string. It should not be necessary to move the whole hand to reach the *D*♯.

Etude

ALLEGRETTO
by Frederick M. Noad

This piece illustrates the importance of attention to right hand fingering, since it can be easy or difficult according to whether this fingering is followed or ignored. Although somewhat unpopular at this stage, particular attention should be given to the *a* finger indications, which will result in much greater smoothness after the necessary practice. Aim for an eventual speed of about ♩ = 120 and a light-hearted style.

A   Prepare the two *C's* with the left hand before commencing.

B   This is an unfamiliar stretch for the left hand at first, but it comes quickly with practice.

C   Be sure to use arpeggio technique here–rest strokes are much too cumbersome in this situation.

D   Leave the 2nd finger on the *E* in preparation for the *E* and *G♯* in the next measure. This makes the chord much easier to find.

Allegretto

Allegretto (continued)

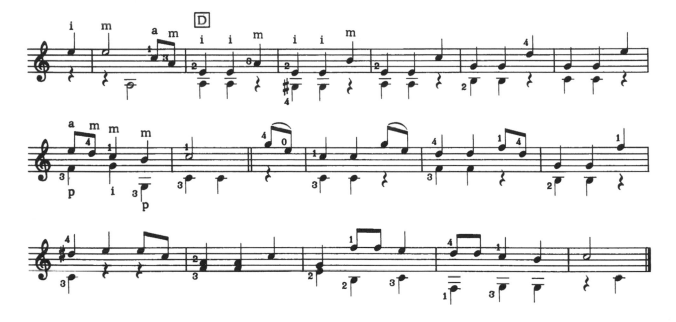

STUDY IN LIGADOS

This study is intended as a thorough practice of ligado technique. It will also demonstrate that ligados can simplify rather than complicate a piece. After practicing it for some days, try playing it through without the ligados and notice how much harder it is to attain a lively speed.

A   Remember to leave the 3rd finger on the *C,* so that it sounds throughout the measure.
B   Leave the 1st finger on in preparation for the *C* in the next measure.
C   Remember to be right on the tip of the little finger here and in similar situations, so that the pull-off movement can be achieved without forcing it.

SARABAND
by Robert De Visée (1686)

Robert de Visée was a court musician to Louis XIV at a time when the guitar, then with five paired strings, reached unprecedented popularity at both the English and French courts.

This piece introduces fuller chords and more advanced movements for the left hand. Aim for a rich, full sound, and be careful to sustain the chords for their full time-value. At this period the Saraband was a slow, stately dance, to be played with grandeur and feeling.

Two-note chords may be slightly arpeggiated, as in *Greensleeves,* and here provide a good contrast to the fuller chords.
A   Leave the 3rd finger on the *A* in preparation for the first chord of the next measure.
B   Extra practice is needed here to make a smooth transition to the chord in the next measure.
C   The wavy line indicates that the chord is to be arpeggiated. This can be done by sweeping the thumb across all the strings. Note that, when chords are involved, the rule of 1st finger 1st fret, 2nd finger 2nd fret, and so on is frequently abandoned, and the 4th finger is frequently used at the 3rd fret.

Study In Ligados

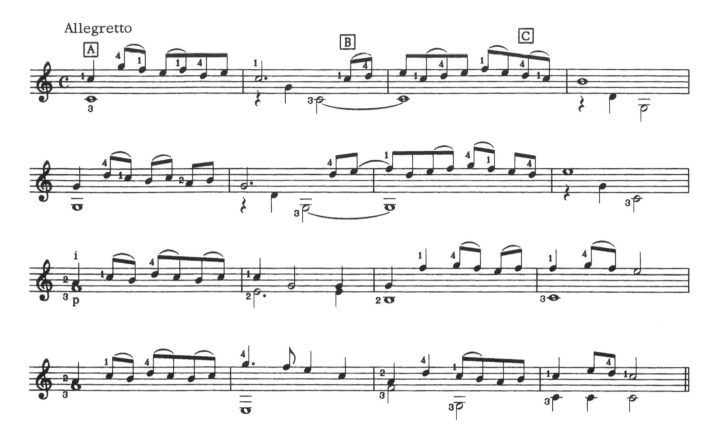

Saraband

MEMORIZATION

To play a piece with complete accuracy and confidence, it is almost essential to commit it to memory. This enables you to watch your left hand and check that the fingers are right up to the frets. It also prevents any division of concentration between the score and the instrument.

When to Memorize

Since memorization of a piece makes it so much easier to play, many people fall into the trap of starting to memorize too soon. For instance, when first approaching a piece they will work out the time and notes for one measure, or perhaps two, and then repeat them until a left hand pattern is established. Then they continue laboriously to the next measure or two and repeat the procedure. The danger here is twofold. First, no overall idea of the piece is acquired to give continuity from one section to another. Second, the music is abandoned so quickly that there is no visual memory of the score, and the notes become so meaningless that a person who has studied a piece this way cannot go *back* to the music when he or she has a memory lapse, since it looks like new material. I have encountered this problem so often, particularly with self-taught players, that I would emphasize strongly the following rule: *Learn to play a piece from beginning to end with absolutely correct fingering and with complete continuity (however slow) before committing it to memory.*

How to Memorize

The most secure memorization is achieved not only by remembering what the fingers do and the shapes and patterns formed on the fingerboard, but also by retaining a visual memory of the score. This is difficult for the beginner at a time when scores are only partly meaningful by themselves, but the formation of good habits at this state will pay tremendous dividends later on. Here is the suggested procedure.

1. Assuming that you have played the piece all the way through a number of times with the music, start at the beginning and see how far you can go without the score.

2. When you have to stop, find the place on the music where you finished, and *without playing* see if you can recognize a few more measures.

3. Put the music away. Now start again, and see how much further you can go. When you stop, repeat the procedure in step 2. Remember that just playing on from the music is not helping you to memorize.

One or more of the pieces in the previous section should be completely memorized before continuing to the next lessons.

DAILY EXERCISES

A routine of daily technique exercises is valuable both for what it achieves and for what it eliminates. A few carefully chosen exercises can replace hours of repetition of old lessons and are the safest guarantee of technical advancement on the instrument. The clearest endorsement of this theory is given by the following true story.

A very famous concert guitarist, whose name is today a household word, was conscripted into the army. Afraid of losing his technique, he evolved an exercise routine covering the main aspects of playing, which could be completed in forty minutes—the maximum time he felt sure of being able to secure daily. After two years of military service, he found that he had not only maintained his ability to play, but actually improved it. As he said afterwards, technique seldom stands still—it either advances or retreats.

A short routine for the player at the present stage follows. If it is practiced conscientiously each day, there is no need to repeat the former lessons.

The exercises are written in the first position since these notes are now familiar, but it is important to follow the instructions about using the other positions on the fingerboard as a preparation for more advanced playing. The patterns are easy to memorize, and this should be done as soon as possible so that the main concentration can be on the hands.

COORDINATION AND PRACTICE
OF REST AND FREE STROKES

Exercise 98

Do not be confused by the number of sharps; the progression of notes is simply demonstrated by the finger numbers, which in this case coincide with the fret numbers.

After playing exercise 98 as written, slide the 1st finger up to the 2nd fret and repeat the pattern. Continue up the fingerboard, starting the pattern on each fret up to and including the 9th. Then repeat exactly the same procedure on the 2nd string, and finally on the 1st.

With the right hand, using first the rest stroke, practice alternating the fingers. After the simple *i m* and *m i* combinations, continue to the more difficult *i a* and finally *m a* alternations. The change may be made to a different alternation when moving to another string.

Speed is not important at first. Concentrate more on evenness of tone quality and rhythm and correctness of technique and position. When starting the first string try to imitate the thicker tone quality of the 3rd and 2nd strings, remembering that the 1st string can sound tinny if care is not taken with the stroke.

After thorough practice with the rest stroke, change to the free stroke, but try to imitate the full tone quality of the rest stroke.

With the left hand, check that the fingers are as vertical as possible to the fingerboard. Pay particular attention to the little finger, which must stop the string on its tip, not on its side. Check that the fingers are right up to the frets.

This is a very comprehensive exercise if used the right way. Just playing the notes is not enough to improve technique; the important thing is to execute the movements as perfectly as possible.

ASCENDING LIGADO (SLUR)

Exercise 99

The basic pattern is shown in the exercise, but note that it begins at the 9th fret of the 3rd string. The reason for this is that the frets are closer together in the higher position, making it easier to do the movements perfectly. After running through the pattern in that position, slide down one fret to the 8th and repeat; then continue at each fret down to the 1st. Complete the exercise by doing the same thing on the 2nd string, then the 1st.

The right hand should practice alternation; use a simple pattern at first so that the main concentration can be on the left hand.

For the left hand it is important, as before, to watch out for the verticality of the fingers and good general position.

DESCENDING LIGADO

Exercise 100

It will be noticed that the pattern for the descending ligado is the same as the previous one but in reverse. The initial position is the same, the first slur being on the 3rd string from the 10th to the 8th fret, and the progression is as before.

When practicing the slur, particular care should be taken with the left hand. Be sure to pull the string down with the finger completing the movement on the fingerboard, not lifted into the air, so that the ligado firmly binds the notes together.

ARPEGGIOS

If the slur exercises have been practiced conscientiously, the left hand will be ready for a rest, so simple chords may be used for the arpeggios, allowing concentration on the right hand.

The number of possible arpeggios is enormous. In his Opus 1, the nineteenth-century composer

Mauro Giuliani gave 120 examples intended for daily practice, and these are reprinted in full in *Solo Guitar Playing,* Book II. The patterns given below should be sufficient at this stage to ensure improvement and muscular development of the right hand.

Exercise 101

Chord Pattern

Exercise 102

Exercise 103

Exercise 104

Exercise 105

Exercise 106

Exercise 107

Exercise 108

Exercise 109

SCALES

The subject of scales is dealt with in greater detail in lesson nineteen, when you will have had more opportunity to learn the notes in the higher positions. At that time you will add diatonic scales to your routine, but for now the following scale passages in different keys will serve to develop your technique without elaborate position changes.

With the right hand use alternation as in exercise 98, practicing rest and free strokes.

Exercise 110

Exercise 111

Exercise 112

Exercise 113

Exercise 114

Exercise 115

Exercise 116

Exercise 117

Exercise 118

Exercise 119

Exercise 120

The Second Position

So far we have confined our attention to the notes of the first four frets, known as the first position. The positions are numbered in accordance with the location of the left hand on the fingerboard by the lowest fret within reach of the 1st finger. For example, the second position embraces all the notes from the 2nd to the 5th fret on each string, the fifth position all the notes from the 5th to the 8th fret.

LEARNING THE SECOND POSITION

To complete the second position it is only necessary to learn the six notes of the 5th fret.

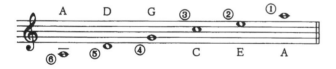

The number in the circle indicates the string. Make a careful note of this way of identifying strings, which now becomes important.

It will be noticed that with one exception (the high *A*) these are all notes that have already been learned in another location. You may wonder why it is necessary to learn the same note in another place. There are two good reasons. First, to avoid unnecessary movement of the left hand up and down the fingerboard, it is often more convenient to use one of these "duplicate" notes than to go back to the 1st position. Second, there is a distinct difference in tone between the same notes played on different strings. For example, play the *E* on the 1st string open. Then play the same note at the 5th

fret of the 2nd string, and notice the difference in quality.

GUIDE FINGERS

There are various ways of changing from one position to another, one of the smoothest and most convenient being the use of a "guide finger." What this means is that after playing a note in one position, the left hand finger slides *without leaving the string* to a fret in the new position, thereby guiding the whole hand to the new location.

In this example the 1st finger moves smoothly from the *G♯* to *A*, taking the hand into the second position. As it moves, the left hand thumb moves with it behind the neck to take up a position behind, or slightly ahead of, the 2nd fret.

Any finger may be used as a guide.

In this example, the hand starts in the second position (indicated by the fact that the 1st, and not the 2nd, finger is on the *A*). The 4th finger, by sliding down to *G♯*, reestablishes the hand in the first position. Note particularly that the thumb must move as the 4th finger slides.

In the following exercises, be sure to decide clearly which position the hand is in and where the changes take place.

Exercise 121

Exercise 122

Exercise 123

Exercise 124

(Folk theme)

Exercise 125

Exercise 126

STUDY NOTES FOR *SONATINA* (duet)
by Thomas Attwood (1765–1838)

Thomas Attwood, a pupil of Mozart, became the organist of St. Paul's Cathedral in 1796. He wrote extensively for the theater as well as the church.

This duet, transcribed from a harpsichord piece, lies well in the second position for which it provides extended and enjoyable practice.

The term *rit* in bar 18 is short for *ritardando,* which means literally holding back, that is, slowing gradually down. It is customary to follow this with a return to strict time, usually marked *a tempo.*

Sonatina

THOMAS ATTWOOD (1765–1838)

Sonatina (continued)

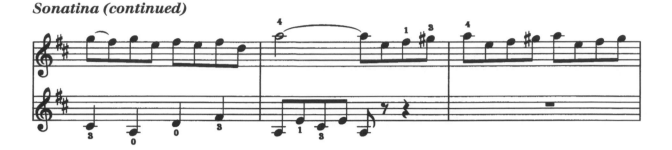

Musical Indications

At the same time as the notes are memorized, it is important to become familiar with the other conventional signs that appear in written music.

DYNAMIC MARKINGS

The normal indications of volume are abbreviations of Italian words. The commonest of these follow.

Indication	Italian word	Meaning
p	*Piano*	Soft
f	*Forte*	Loud
cresc, or ◁	*Crescendo*	Growing louder
dim, or ▷	*Diminuendo*	Growing softer

Various gradations can be indicated from *pp* (very soft) through *mp* and *mf* (moderately soft, moderately loud) to *ff* (very loud).

Accentuation of particular notes is shown by either ⌃ or ⌐. A sharp separation of notes, in extreme contrast to the ligado, is known as *staccato* playing, indicated by a dot above or below the notes concerned.

TEMPO INDICATIONS

Indications of speed are also normally given in Italian, the most usual being

Indication	Speed	Literal meaning
Largo	Very slow	Broad
Lento	Slow	Slow
Adagio	Slow	At ease
Andante	Fairly slow	Walking pace
Moderato	Moderate speed	Moderate
Allegro	Fairly fast	Gay
Vivace	Brisk	Lively
Presto	Fast	Fast

A gradual slowing down, quite frequent at the end of a piece, is indicated by the term *rallentando* or *ritardando*. These are usually abbreviated to *rall.* or *rit.* The opposite, an increase in speed, is indicated by *accelerando* or *accel.*

A pause, or slight extra hold to a note, is indicated by the *fermata*, which is drawn thus: 𝄐.

COUNTING SIXTEENTH NOTES

As the faster notes are approached, it becomes more difficult to find a "syllabic" method of counting, and various systems exist. Perhaps the simplest is to become accustomed to breaking the number counts and *ands* into two syllables, making in each case two sounds where previously there was one and thus giving the time for the sixteenth note. For instance, four sixteenth notes at the beginning of a measure would be counted

Of course the four sounds must be made as even as, for instance, four quick taps on a table. The advantage over systems that use other words or syllables for sixteenth notes is that it is still possible to be sure which beat of the measure is being counted.

Here are some further examples. Try playing as well as counting them. For clarity all the half-beat *ands* are included.

DAMPING

Notes should not be left to ring beyond their correct time value, particularly when followed by a rest or a chord with which they are discordant. In most cases it is necessary to release the pressure of only the left hand finger from the fret, but when open strings are involved it is more usual to use the right hand.

The most useful right hand method of damping is simply to drop the side of the thumb onto the strings. This can be done on the lower strings without putting the hand out of position and is thus particularly useful in the middle of a piece where continuity must not be lost.

To silence the guitar completely, the right hand may be stretched out and the palm laid across all the strings.

Exercise 127

The Third Position

The sooner the notes on the fingerboard are thoroughly learned, the sooner it is possible to approach the more interesting pieces in the guitar repertoire. Often these pieces do not present great technical difficulty, and the only necessity is a thorough knowledge of the notes in the positions concerned.

Again it is only necessary to learn six new notes to complete the third position, which extends from the 3rd to the 6th fret. Here are the new notes—all at the 6th fret.

As with the second position, remember that the whole hand must move with the guide finger. The exercises should be repeated until the new position and fingerings are thoroughly familiar.

THE HALF BAR

Sometimes it is convenient to stop more than one string with the 1st finger of the left hand. To do this it is necessary to place the finger flat across the required strings, known as "barring." When the finger covers all the strings, this is known as a "full bar." When a lesser number are covered, the term "half bar" is used, an expression that is slightly misleading as the half bar may comprise from two to five strings, and not just three strings as the word "half" would imply.

The half bar shown in the illustration covers the 1st, 2nd, and 3rd and 4th strings. Note that the finger is close to the fret, which can just be felt by the finger. The pressure should be evenly exerted over the four strings.

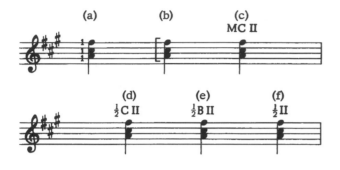

(a)   (b)   (c)
MC II

(d)   (e)   (f)
½C II   ½B II   ½ II

a. The fingering indication shows that the 1st finger must cover all three notes.

b. The bracket line indicates the notes to be barred.

c. The letters *MC* are abbreviated from the Spanish *medio capotasto,* meaning "half bar."

d. *d, e,* and *f* are self-explanatory and used according to the nationality of the editor. This author prefers the use of *f,* which gives the fullest information as briefly as possible.

While the 1st finger holds the half bar, other fingers may play, and the duration of the half bar is usually indicated by a line or dotted line.

EXERCISE NOTES

These exercises are all fingered in the third position, and this fingering should be carefully observed, or the point of them is lost. String indications are given in exercise 128. After that it is left to you. In exercise 129, in the third measure, notice that the 4th finger is used on the high *A.* This does *not* mean a move to the second position–the 4th finger is often used like this to avoid jumping the same finger from one string to another. However, in the fifth measure a brief move is made back to the second position because that *A* cannot be played in the third. The 3rd finger slides to the *C* at the beginning of the next measure to reestablish the hand in the third position.

In exercise 133 the 4 sixteenth notes in the first measure are played ligado. Play the *F,* then pull off to sound the *E* and *D,* then hammer the final *E.*

Be sure to practice the half bars where indicated.

Exercise 128

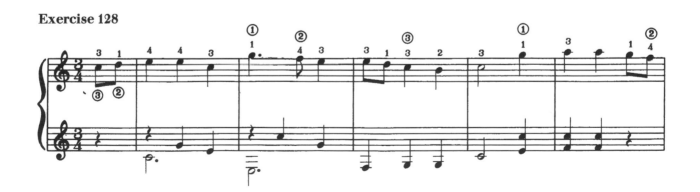

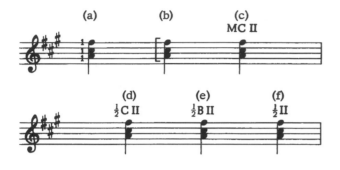

Exercise 128 (continued)

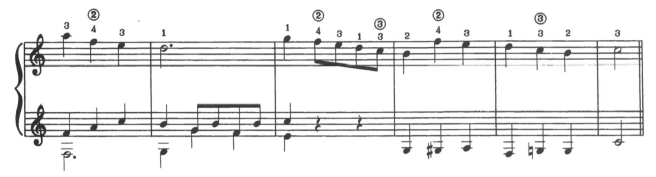

Exercise 129

Exercise 130

Exercise 131

Exercise 132

Exercise 132 (continued)

Exercise 133

Exercise 134

(Folk Song "Waly Waly")

Third position except as noted

New Time Signatures

Up to this point all counting has been based on the quarter note as the unit for each count. In cases where the lower figure in the time signature is not a four but another number, the note represented by that number becomes the counting unit. For instance, in 3/8 or 6/8 time the eighth note is the counting reference, and the measures contain three and six counts respectively. In 3/2 time the half note becomes the unit for counting, and the measure contains three counts of a half note duration.

COUNTING IN EIGHTH NOTES

Counting with the eighth note as the unit presents no particular problem, as long as it is remembered that the other notes must be doubled in value, that is, the quarter note has two counts, the dotted quarter note three counts, etc. Sixteenth notes can be counted using the *and* device previously used to count eighth notes. The dotted eighth note is counted exactly like the dotted quarter note in 4/4 time, that is, *one (and) two.*

Here is an example in 3/8 time.

1 2 3   1 &2 & 3   1   2 &3 &   1 2 3

Play the example counting as indicated until you are sure *why* each count is where it is.

SIX-EIGHT TIME

When approaching 6/8 time, the question arises, "Why not use 3/4 time, since six eighth notes last the same length of time as three quarter notes?" The answer lies in the rhythm. Characteristically 6/8 time has two groups of three eighth notes with a stress on the 1st and 4th counts.

<u>1</u> 2 3 <u>4</u> 5 6   <u>1</u> 2 3 <u>4</u> 5 6   <u>1</u> 2 3 <u>4</u> 5 6   <u>1</u> 2 3 <u>4</u> 5 6

If you counted this passage in 3/4 time it would produce stresses in the wrong places.

Eighth Note Counting

Counting in eighth notes may be used sometimes for 3/4 or 4/4 time to clarify particularly difficult rhythms.

1   2   3   4 & 5   6 & 7   8 &

In principle, however, when the time has been deciphered it is better to revert to the quarter note count.

Now try the piece that follows for practice in 6/8 time. Where necessary count out the music before playing.

STUDY NOTES FOR *RONDO*
by Ferdinando Carulli

The feeling of two beats as in the bass line, as well as the six eighth note beats in the upper part, demonstrates the meaning of "compound time." Each measure contains two groups of three, with an accent on the first of each group. Other examples of compound time are $\frac{6}{4}$, in which there are two groups of 3 quarter notes, or $\frac{9}{8}$ with three groups of 3 eighth notes.

The feeling of two beats becomes apparent as you bring the piece up to tempo, which should be fairly brisk to give the feel of a country dance.

Rondo

TEST NUMBER THREE

1. What frets could be reached in the 5th position?

2. What is the purpose of a guide finger?

3. Play the following notes (all within the first six frets):

On the 1st string *G*♯

On the 2nd string *F*

On the 3rd string *B*

On the 4th string *G*

On the 5th string *C*♯

On the 6th string *A*♯

4. What is the difference in counting the dotted quarter note between $\frac{3}{4}$ and $\frac{3}{8}$ time?

5. How many strings are covered by the half bar?

6. What are the rules of memorization?

7. Play from memory at least two of the pieces from the section following lesson twelve.

8. Play from memory all daily exercises.

9. Write the correct count under the following passages:

10. Fill in rests where necessary in the following example:

NINE PIECES WITH STUDY NOTES

CANARY JIG
(*Canarios*)

This dance was very popular in the seventeenth century in both France and Spain, and versions exist by Couperin, Purcell, Sanz, Ribayaz, and others. It was reputedly based on a dance of the natives of the Canary Islands.

It should be played with a brisk, lively rhythm and should not present much difficulty, provided that care is taken with the right hand fingering at *A*.

Canary Jig

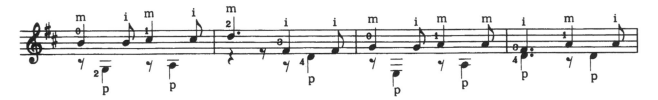

MINUET
by Robert De Visée

Originally of country origin the minuet became an extremely popular dance at the court of Louis XIV, after its introduction by the composer Lully. De Visée was a great admirer of Lully (who also played the guitar) and made no secret of trying to imitate his style.

The *Minuet* shown here should be played with grace, but not fast. Suggested tempo is ♩ = 116.

A   For this fingering of the *A* chord, the first finger covers both the 3rd and 4th strings but is raised to clear to the top open string. If unfamiliar at first it will be found with practice to be a very useful fingering in that it leaves the 3rd and 4th fingers to play without disturbing the chord.

Minuet

BOURRÉE
by Robert De Visée

The *Bourrée* was a French country dance that became popular with composers toward the end of the seventeenth century. Characteristically it begins with an up-beat (the last beat of an incomplete measure) and is played at a lively tempo.

This piece should make a contrast with the preceding *Minuet,* with a tempo of about ♩ = 144 as a final target. It is not easy but is extremely effective when well played.

A The ligado from 4th to 2nd finger should receive extra practice.

B Leave the first finger on the *C* in preparation for the first chord of the next measure.

C The use of the 4th finger as a guide is the only way to negotiate this passage up to tempo.

D A very quick change must be made here to the third position.

In general, if the individual measures with problems are practiced separately, this will be found to be a rewarding piece.

Bourrée

THEME
by G. F. Handel (1685–1759)

This theme is commonly known as the "Harmonious Blacksmith," and it is a good example of how much music can come from only two parts. Aim at a tempo of about ♩ = 92, and try to keep a feeling of continuity.

A Extra practice is needed here for the change into the second position.

B Here the 2nd, 4th, and 3rd fingers should go on together. If necessary, first practice placing the 2nd and 3rd fingers, both at the fourth fret, then add the little finger.

C The 3rd finger on the C♯ here releases the 1st and 2nd fingers in preparation for the chord that follows.

In general this piece is a little harder than it appears at first sight, but methodical practice of it will produce improved stretch and facility of the left hand.

Theme

BOURRÉE
by J. S. Bach (1685–1750)

It is important to follow the fingering very carefully in this piece, as the hand moves frequently from first to second position. Originally for unaccompanied cello, this dance should be lively in character, with a final speed of about ♩ = 132.

A The 1st finger on the *A* establishes the hand in the second position. Be sure that the left hand thumb is in the correct place and not lagging in the first position.

B The placement of the half bar here presents the principal difficulty of the piece. Without taking the 1st finger from the *A*, practice laying the finger down to cover the *C♯*. Then move the 3rd finger over to the *C♯* on the 5th string, holding the half bar so that the final *A* of the measure is prepared.

C The crossing of the 2nd finger over the 1st will seem strange at first, but this ensures that the 1st finger is in position to start the repeat or the second section.

D Again a cross-fingering–awkward, but it is important to sustain the *F♯* for its full value.

E Leave the 2nd finger on the *D* in preparation for the *D* in the next measure. This takes the difficulty out of finding the chord that follows.

F Work out the scale passage methodically and give it extra practice.

Bourrée

PEZZO TEDESCO
Anonymous

This lute piece from the Italian renaissance is taken from a collection transcribed from the original lute tablature by the nineteenth-century musicologist Oscar Chilesotti. The title means literally "German Dance," and a contemporary description of this form shows it to have had uncomplicated steps and probably a moderate tempo.

A Be careful with the right hand fingering here and avoid playing the open *B* string.

B Try to keep this succession of chords accurate without grabbing with the left hand. In general the piece affords good opportunities for improving chord changes–remember to make minimal movements with both hands.

Pezzo Tedesco

ORLANDO SLEEPETH
by John Dowland (1563–1626)

John Dowland was the leading lutenist-composer of the very fruitful Elizabethan period in England. The piece is straightforward and descriptive and should be played slowly with a slight increase in tempo for the $\frac{6}{4}$ section.

A   The half bar here enables you to sustain the *A* for its full time-value.

B   Although slightly unusual, the 3rd finger on the *C♯* facilitates a smooth chord change.

It is effective to play the first section moderately loud, with the repeat very soft and in the nature of an echo.

Orlando Sleepeth

MRS. WINTER'S JUMP
by John Dowland

In contrast to the dreaming mood of the previous piece, *Mrs. Winter's Jump* is a lively dance tune.

This version was published in 1596 for the Orpharion, a steel-stringed plucked instrument tuned similarly to the modern guitar.

The tempo should be brisk and lively, in keeping with the title.

Mrs. Winter's Jump

AIR
by Thomas Robinson (1603)

It was a common practice in the Elizabethan period for lutenist-composers to take a popular melody and embellish it in their own particular style. The song in this case was about Robin Hood, entitled "Robin Is to the Greenwood Gone." The first four measures represent the first line of the song, which is then elaborated slightly for the next four measures. The succeeding eight measures are treated in the same way by being repeated in more complex rhythm.

Great care is needed in counting this piece, which should be practiced to an eventual metronome speed of about ♩ = 80.

A   A difficult chord, but the use of the 3rd finger as a guide greatly facilitates the change. The *D* is of course on the 5th string.

B   The scale here is typical and really serves to fill the measure since the chord would not sustain this long. It should be played lightly and without emphasis.

C   Practice is needed here for a smooth transition to the third position.

D   The open *E* covers the move of the hand up to the second position.

E   Try not to rush this position change. Move the 4th finger with precision to the 5th fret, allowing the hand to travel with it.

Air

MUSICIANSHIP

So far the lessons have been concerned with the technique of playing notes and reading music. When the basic problems of technique are overcome, it is important to remember that the object of playing a musical instrument is not to execute notes, but to make music. Music is a means of expression and communication, and for this reason has often been called a language. Like spoken language it is divided into the equivalent of phrases, sentences, and paragraphs, and it is important to try to see these, so that a musical performance becomes a coherent statement. Again following the same parallel, when we speak, we use our voices in varying pitch and volume, since we know that a monotone is unexpressive and boring.

Without introducing undue complexity, there are certain simple steps that may be followed to produce a more musical rendering of a piece. First, check the given information at the beginning of the piece. Very often the title is an indication of the general character of the music and is the first point to consider. If the title is "Air," "Song Tune," "Aria," etc., it is clear that the composer means the piece to be lyrical and vocal in character. If, on the contrary, the title is that of a dance form, such as "Minuet," "Jig," "Waltz," etc., then a strict rhythmic approach is indicated. The next indication is the tempo marking, which sometimes conveys more than a bare statement of speed. For instance, the indication *lento maestoso,* meaning literally "slow and majestic," gives an immediate clue to the type of performance required.

The next step is to consider the dynamic markings. If they are those of the composer, they should be carefully noted and respected. If they are merely the suggestions of an editor, they may be changed for good reason but should at least be given consideration. Remember that the guitar is not an instrument of great volume and that it is particularly important to use such dynamic range as it does have. When a section is repeated, it may, to good effect, often be played loud the first time and soft on the repeat, thereby making a passage musically interesting, instead of merely repetitive.

Having absorbed the given information, it is time to experiment. Try to see the statements that the music is making, and particularly do not hurry from one section to another. One of the most common faults of students is the shortening of a long note at the end of a phrase in an anxiety to reach the next note without a silence intervening. The result is a hurried, nervous-sounding performance. The experienced musician gives long notes their full duration and is not afraid to let the music "breathe," that is, leave just a hint of a pause at the end of a section as if taking a breath.

Another great aid to an interesting performance is the full use of the tonal variety of the guitar. This subject is discussed in detail in lesson eighteen.

Finally, remember that one of the best ways to increase knowledge and understanding of music is by intelligent listening. Although nothing is better than a good live performance, cassettes and CDs can bring the world's greatest musicians to you, and they are frequently loaned out by public libraries. It is a good idea to compare different performances of the same piece to see how two musicians can take quite a different view of a piece, and yet each produce an excellent interpretation. Listening should not be confined solely to the guitar—there is much to be learned from other instrumentalists.

The steps outlined here are easy to take, and it cannot be too strongly recommended that the serious student make every effort from the earliest stages to be not only a guitarist but a musician as well.

The Fifth Position

As you learn the higher notes on the fingerboard, not only do better pieces become approachable but also more tonal variation can be attained because of the availability of equivalent notes on different strings.

Some positions are convenient for simple keys with few sharps or flats; others lend themselves more naturally to the complex keys. For this reason the fifth position is studied before the fourth, which is more suitable for keys with many sharps.

Changing from the first to the fifth position requires a more extensive movement of the left hand, and the simple slide of a guide finger is more often replaced by a "through" movement.

In this example the *C* and *D* are played on the 2nd string in the first position. The 1st finger remains on the string until the *D* has been played, then slides through to the 5th fret, without losing contact with the string, to play the *E* and establish the hand in the fifth position.

Frequently an open string enables the hand to change position smoothly.

In this passage the open *E* is sounding as the hand moves up to play the *A* and establish the fifth position.

NOTES IN THE FIFTH POSITION

To learn the position thoroughly start with the "white notes" (i.e., those without sharps or flats). After these are thoroughly memorized it is easy to fill in the gaps.

Note that the position contains all the notes from *A* below the staff to *C* above it, with the exception of the *B* in the center of the staff. If the hand is to remain in the fifth position, this note may be played on the 2nd string open.

The following exercises are progressive in difficulty and should be well studied for familiarity with the position.

EXERCISE NOTES

As before, string indications are given in the first exercise only. After that keep the hand in the fifth position and use the fingering to discover the right string.

In exercise 136 the open *B* string is used, but the hand remains in the fifth position. The triplet in the seventh measure should be counted *four-and-a* and played ligado.

The last part of exercise 137 also uses the open *B* to allow the hand to remain in the fifth position.

Note that in this position the 4th finger is sometimes used at the 7th fret to avoid awkward jumps with the 3rd finger.

In exercise 139 the hand moves down to the first position for the last two measures of each section. Otherwise, it remains in the fifth position throughout.

Exercise 135

Exercise 136

Exercise 137

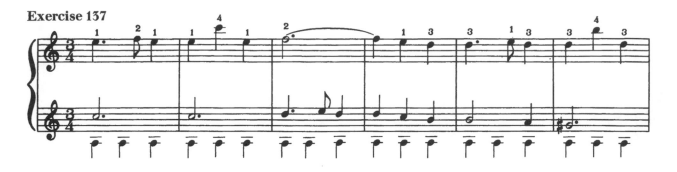

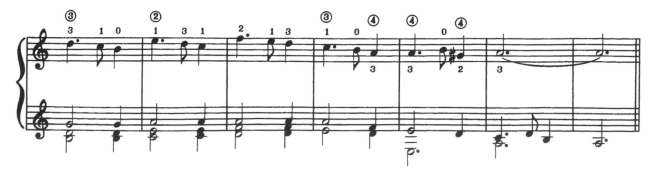

Exercise 138
(Catalan folk song)

Exercise 139

(Irish Tune "Lilliburlero")

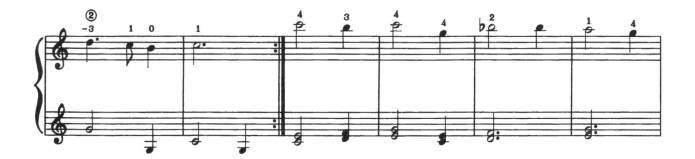

Exercise 140

The Full Bar

This lesson returns to the subject of technique, introducing one of the most useful devices for extending the playing possibilities of the left hand–the full bar.

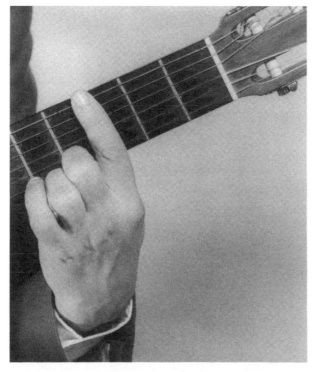

RULES FOR FORMING THE FULL BAR

The illustration shows the position for the complete bar covering all strings. Note carefully the following rules:

1. The left hand should exert the *minimum* pressure sufficient to produce clear notes.

2. Do not let the fingertip project unnecessarily beyond the fingerboard.

3. Be sure that the crease below the final joint of the finger does not coincide with the 4th string. For most people it will be possible to position this crease between the 3rd and 4th strings, without losing contact with the 6th string.

4. The finger should be right up to the fret and just able to feel it.

5. The finger is not completely flat across the strings, but angled slightly counterclockwise, looking at the fingertip. However, this should not be exaggerated as that would limit the stretch of the other fingers.

FIRST EXERCISE FOR THE FULL BAR

As a first practice, and to ensure minimum pressure, try the following.

1. Place the left hand 1st finger in the position to bar at the 2nd fret, but just touching the strings and without pressing them down.

2. Sweep across the strings with the thumb of the right hand. The notes should be muted.

3. Gradually press down the left hand finger, continuously sweeping across the strings with the right hand just to the point where clear notes are sounded. This gives an indication of the minimum pressure for the bar.

4. Repeat the experiment at the 5th, 7th, and other frets. The aim should be to produce a clear sound from each string without undue pressure of the left hand.

The bar is indicated by a Roman numeral, which may be preceded by either *C* (Capotasto) or *B* (Barré). As with the half bar, it should be held for the length of the line or dotted line.

The next exercise draws on Spanish flamenco and provides an excellent practice study for the full bar. When played up to time, it has an impressive sound hinting at virtuoso technique.

Here also is an example of both simple and compound time, a mixture typical of idiomatic Spanish music. The $\frac{3}{2}$ is counted *one* and *two* and *three* and, with stress on the number beats. In contrast the $\frac{6}{4}$ is counted *one* two three *four* *five six*, with stress on beats *one* and *four*.

The tempo will be governed by the sixteenth notes, which must relate correctly to the slower notes in the opening.

Small self-contained segments such as this are known as "falsetas," and a typical flamenco piece consists of a series of these put together according to the taste of the performer.

Exercise 141

(La Caña)

FIVE PIECES WITH STUDY NOTES

DOVE SON QUEI FIERI OCCHI
Anonymous

The next three pieces are taken from Chilesotti's collection of lute pieces from the Italian renaissance. The fingering takes advantage of the new positions for smoother changes and greater tonal variety. Although harder to read than pieces in the lower positions, they should not present much technical difficulty once memorized.

A The *C* is played on the third string at the 5th fret. Then both the 3rd and 4th fingers move up two frets to the *B* and *D*.

B This fingering provides the smoothest transition to the *C* and *A* and back to the barred chord. Do not be tempted to go back to the first position.

C Great care should be taken to finger this measure correctly. Note that the *D* is taken on the 5th string and that the 2nd finger then slides up the same string to find the *E* at the 7th fret. The final *A* is taken on the 4th string, ensuring a smooth change to the first chord of the next measure.

D The *G* in this chord is played on the 4th string to make the ligado possible and also to emphasize this voice.

Dove Son Quei Fieri Occhi

SE IO M'ACCORGO
Anonymous

The tempo here should be about ♩= 120. Do not be tempted to hurry the chords at the beginning. Let them ring clearly for their full time value.

A   The use of the 4th string for the A and G gives a consistent and rich sound to this voice.

B   Notice that the upper voice enters here with the same melody. This is known as a "canon" movement. It is particularly important to sustain the long notes in the lower voice so that the melody is continuous.

C   This passage is an echolike reminder of the melody. The A is taken at the 10th fret of the 2nd string for tonal variety. The 4th finger then slides to the G at the 8th fret, establishing the hand in the fifth position.

D   This section is played as follows: Play the A and low E with p and m. Then pull off the A to sound the G♯. Hammer the A on again with the 2nd finger, and again pull off to sound the G♯. Do this once more to sound the A and G♯ again, then play the final F♯ and G♯ with i and m. Note that from the initial chord until the F♯ the right hand does not play, the notes being sounded by the left hand ligado movements.

ITALIANA
Anonymous

Italiana was a very popular tune in the sixteenth century, and several different versions of it can be found. It should be played as a lively dance with strict rhythm and an eventual tempo of about ♩= 176.

A   The common tendency here and at similar points is to hurry the first note of each slurred pair. To counteract this, give a slight extra stress to the first notes. This will result in better ligados and more even tempo.

B   Accent the G here, and be sure to hold it through to the next measure.

C   In the succeeding sixteen measures, practice the right hand fingering as carefully as the left to take the difficulty out of this passage.

D   Slow down the tempo here to make the ending decisive.

Se Io M'accorgo

Italiana

6th string to D

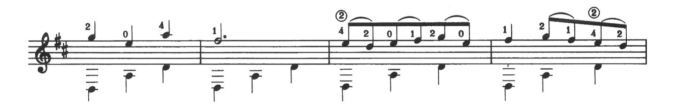

Italiana (continued)

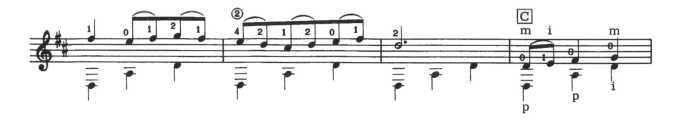

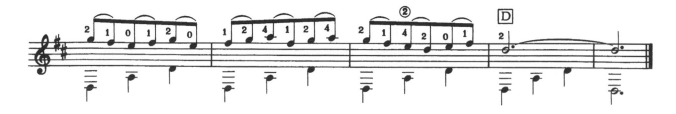

PAVANE
by Luis Milan (1535)

The Pavane was a slow stately dance, which probably originated in the Italian town of Padua, though some attribute its origin to the Spanish word *pavo,* meaning peacock. In his book *The Maestro,* Milan described this piece as one written in the style of the Italian "pavane." The melody was from Italy, but the arrangement by Milan. The general style should be majestic with a metronome setting of about 80 for the half notes.

A   The fingering of these two chords is important, the 2nd finger acting as a guide up to and back from the third position bar.

B   The 4th finger is necessary as a guide to the difficult chord that follows.

C   Play this measure loud, with a soft echo for the next measure.

D   The 4th finger here indicates a move back to the first position.

E   Play the $F\sharp$ strongly enough to sustain the melody through to the G.

In general aim for a positive performance with every note clearly defined. Make the chords ring, and vary the dynamics to sustain interest.

ETUDE IN D
by Fernando Sor (1778–1839)

Fernando Sor was the leading guitarist-composer of his day. In addition to touring in concert through all the main capitals of Europe, he was a prolific composer of both concert pieces and didactic studies.

This study should be played lightly and with grace. Aim for a tempo of about $\quarternote = 112$. As with all studies, every note is important and should be clearly audible in the finished version. A pattern of right hand fingering is given in the first part, and this should be followed for the remainder of the piece.

A   Accent the dotted quarter notes to bring out the melody

B   A problem spot: Bar three strings at the first fret, then without lifting the 1st finger, ease the bar up to the second position.

C   The last joint of the 1st finger covers both the A and E. The finger may be turned slightly backwards onto its side to facilitate this.

D   The 1st finger here indicates a sudden change to the third position. This movement should be practiced for smoothness.

E   Here also there is a sudden change of position, but the open E gives the opportunity for the hand to move.

Pavane

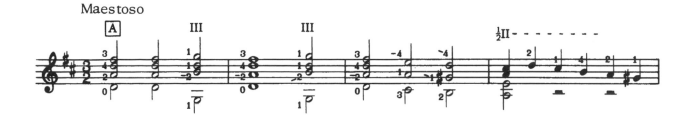

Etude in D

Allegro grazioso

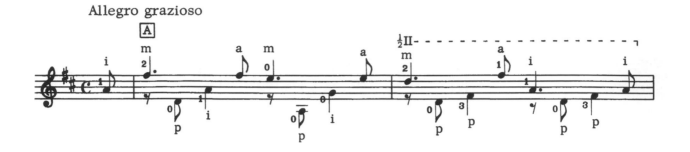

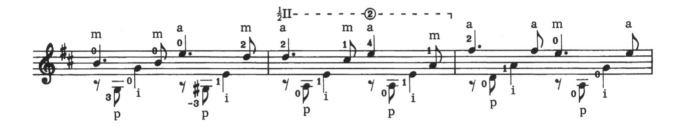

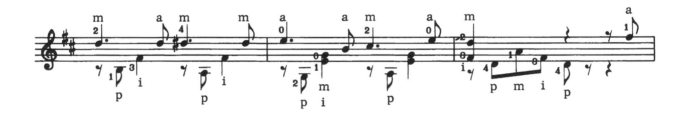

Etude in D (continued)

TONE PRODUCTION

One of the most compelling attractions of the guitar is the singularly sweet and sensitive tone that can be produced from it. Of course the quality of the instrument is important, but a surprisingly beautiful sound can be produced from the humblest of guitars. In general, students tend to spend considerable time and money trying to find a guitar with the ultimate sound instead of working on the techniques of tone production.

VIBRATO

The principal technique of the left hand for producing tonal variation is known as "vibrato." The effect of this is to alter the pitch very slightly so that the note wavers, resulting in a more emotional sound. There are two ways to produce this variation in pitch, and an approximate rule can be formulated according to the position on the fingerboard.

Frets 1–4 and 13–19

In the first position and above the 12th fret, vibrato can be produced by pushing the string rapidly from side to side without releasing the pressure of the left hand.

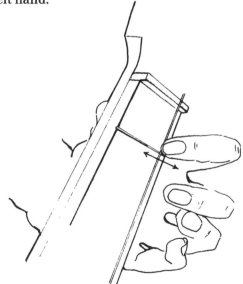

Great care must be taken with this type of vibrato, so as not to exaggerate the variation in pitch. If done to excess, the result is a wailing sound more appropriate to the "blues" than to the classical repertoire. As a technique it is used sparingly, and chiefly because the normal vibrato described next is less effective at these frets.

Frets 5–12

In this area of the guitar a type of vibrato can be used that is comparable to the technique used by other stringed instrument players. Again, without releasing pressure on the string, the left hand oscillates in the plane shown by the diagram. The slight pull and push of the string along its length produces a small and wavering vibration of pitch.

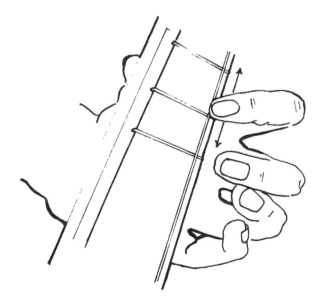

Although harder to do effectively at first, this type of vibrato is on the whole more satisfying as it is unlikely to be excessive. For experimental purposes while learning, it is more easily produced on the 2nd, 4th, 5th, and 6th strings.

USING VIBRATO

Some players reserve the vibrato for use as a special effect to intensify or add emotion to a passage.

Others, like most violinists nowadays, use it by habit as a basic part of their technique. In general this does not sound excessive, since the vibrato cannot be used on chords of more than two notes or during fast passages. However, a general habit of using the first type of vibrato is not recommended for the reasons mentioned earlier.

The period of vibration of the hand in forming the vibrato can be varied for different effects and is one of the factors that contribute to the individuality of a player's tone.

OTHER LEFT HAND TECHNIQUES

Distinct from the ligado there are two other methods of linking notes in sound to produce a smoother or more vocal effect. There are many names for these, but probably the most convenient are "portamento" and "slide."

The Portamento

Originally a term applied to singing, the portamento literally means the "carrying" of one note to another through the intermediate pitches. This is imitated on the guitar by playing a note, then moving the same left hand finger to the next note without reducing pressure on the fingerboard, thereby sounding the intervening tones before playing the second note. The portamento, like the vibrato, is very rarely indicated in guitar music since it is considered an effect best left to the good taste of the player. It is most appropriate in slow passages of lyrical style, but it may often be used in conjunction with a guide finger to assist a smooth change of position.

portamento   Effect.
fingering.

The Slide

In contrast to the portamento, the slide is marked in the music and is employed where a more extreme effect is required, usually covering a wide interval of notes.

This example is executed on the third string. After the *B* is played, the 4th finger slides quickly up the fingerboard, maintaining pressure on it and coming to a dead stop behind the 13th fret. Note that the left hand alone sounds the high *G♯*.

If the right hand is to play the final note, this can be indicated by drawing a small grace note beside the final note of the slide.

The slide should be distinguished from the "glissando" as follows: The slide is executed by a fast continuous movement of the left hand, which gives an impression of the notes in between but is too quick to sound them individually. The *glissando*, in contrast, sounds the succession of notes individually in the form of a fast scale and necessitates a minute pause of the left hand at each fret. This technique is extremely rare in guitar music.

The slide was more popular at the end of the last century than it is today, and it should be mentioned that many of the slides appearing in the music of that period are converted by modern players into *portamenti*. When they appear before a note as a form of grace note, they are also frequently omitted altogether.

RIGHT HAND TECHNIQUES

Obviously of major importance to the production of good tone with the right hand is the shape and condition of the nails. If these are too long, speed is impaired. If they are too short, it is difficult to control the strokes. A certain amount of individual experimentation is necessary since the shape and size of fingers and nails vary; but as a general rule when looking at the right hand, palm forward, a ridge of nail should be visible over the tops of the fingers, extending about 1/16 inch and following the shape of the fingertips. Pointed nails should be avoided, as should sharp corners at the extreme sides of the nails.

The smoothness of the nail is as important as its shape. After a nail is filed it usually produces an unpleasant scratchy tone, which may persist for two days or more. Methods of overcoming this include the use of the finest grade of sandpaper to smooth the surface or of a type of fine abrasive stone known as *Arkansas stone*, which is normally used to sharpen very fine tools.

The angle of attack of the fingernail has a strong influence on the type of sound produced. If the finger is at right angles to the string, the maximum amount of nail is in contact at the beginning of the stroke suitable for emphatic, loud playing. A more

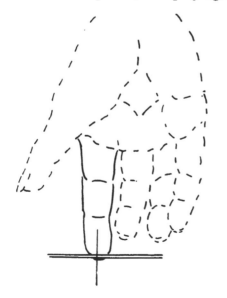

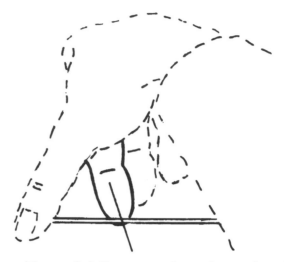

sensitive and delicate sound can be produced by angling the finger so that only part of the nail is engaged.

CONTINUITY OF SOUND

In a fast passage a small period of silence between notes would be scarcely perceptible. However, in a slow melodic line, care must be taken not to damp the notes before their time-value is completed. This can best be seen by an example.

If the *m* finger commences with a rest stroke, the *i* finger must be held away from the string until the last possible moment. Then it must come down with sufficient velocity so that there is no appreciable break in sound. In turn the *m* finger must remain poised until the half note *F* is completed.

Although this may seem an obvious point, it is mentioned because so many students have a tendency to prepare the succeeding note in advance, producing in effect something like this:

The result is decidedly not lyrical.

TONE CONTRASTS

Apart from the nail angle variation mentioned earlier, the main changes in tone color are made by moving the right hand nearer to the bridge or the fingerboard.

Playing closer to the bridge, the sound is more metallic and is sometimes referred to as the harpsichord effect. In the music it is indicated by the words *metallico* or *sul ponticello* (literally *on the bridge*). Note particularly that this effect should be handled using free strokes since the rest strokes produce a hard and unpleasant sound in this position.

In complete contrast is the sound produced by playing close to the fingerboard. This is sometimes indicated as *sul diapason,* or, more usually simply *dolce* (sweet). The tone is rounder and sweeter, and this is even more accentuated if the passage is fingered in the higher positions. Compare the following:

1) *Sul ponticello*, free stroke.

2) *Dolce*, rest strokes.

CONCLUSION

The techniques described here can be used in varying degrees and combinations to produce an exceptionally wide range of sounds and effects. In this respect the guitarist has a great advantage over, for instance, the pianist, and it is important to recognize and use this additional means of expression. When attention is given to good tone production and variation, a player develops a completely individual sound, and it is interesting to note that between the best soloists there is such a surprising difference of tone, which has very little to do with the instruments that they are playing. Above all, the student is recommended to experiment without fear of exaggeration. It is always more interesting to hear effects and contrasts slightly overdone than to hear a timid or unimaginative monotone.

Scales

The subject of scales is often a somewhat unwelcome one to the student since it is associated with boring practice drills or unnecessary academicism. However, scales are particularly useful to the guitarist, both for overcoming technique problems in both hands and also as a help to understanding the relationship between different keys and modes. In his preface to an edition of major and minor scales Andrés Segovia wrote "The practice of scales enables one to solve a greater number of technical problems in a shorter time than the study of any other exercise."

THE CHROMATIC SCALE

In the simplest form of scale the notes move by successive half-tones (one fret on the guitar). This is known as a chromatic scale.

Such a scale could be played on the guitar by simply advancing up a string one fret at a time and is quite useful as an exercise in smooth through movements. For instance, it may be played on the 3rd string as follows:

Then it may be repeated on the 2nd and 1st strings following the same fret pattern.

It is easy to hear that such a progression of notes in a melody would become exceedingly dull, and for melodic purposes the most commonly used progressions of notes are taken from the major and minor scales.

THE MAJOR SCALE

If we play the succession of notes from *C* on the 5th string to *C* on the 2nd string without sharps or flats, we have in fact played a major scale. It will be noticed that the interval between the notes is sometimes a whole tone (two frets on the guitar) and sometimes a half tone (one fret on the guitar).

In the major scale the half-tones fall between the third and fourth and the seventh and eighth notes. This form of scale has found favor with composers and become an accepted tradition in Western music. In the Orient, different scales are in more common usage, giving a different flavor or characteristic to the music. The scale is named by the note on which it starts and finishes, the previous being the major scale of *C*, or as it is more commonly known, the scale of *C* Major.

A major scale can be formed on any other note simply by preserving the same intervals.

In the last example the scale starts on *G*. The same intervals must be used, and since *B* to *C* is a half-tone the first part of the scale presents no problem. However the seventh to the eighth note must also be a half-tone, and this can only be achieved by sharping the *F*. Hence in the *G* Major scale the *F* is always sharped, and this is indicated at the beginning of the musical line.

SCALES AND KEYS

The relationship between scales and keys is a very simple one. A melody that uses the notes of the *C* Major scale is said to be in the key of *C* Major. A melody using the notes of the *G* Major scale is in the key of *G* Major and consequently will have the *F* sharped throughout. This indication at the beginning of each line is known as the "key signature."

THE MINOR SCALES

The simplest form of minor scale may be played by sounding the notes from the open *A* (5th string) to the *A* on the 3rd string in succession with no sharps or flats. This form of scale is known as the "natural minor."

This scale was later modified in various ways to suit the needs or customs of composers. For instance, from the harmonic point of view, composers tended to prefer the progression:

to the same thing with a *G* natural, particularly at the end of a piece. To accommodate this the scale was written sharping the *G*. This became known as the "harmonic" minor scale.

The only disadvantage in this scale was that the interval from *F* to *G♯* was somewhat awkward to sing, such an interval being more characteristic of Middle Eastern music. This problem was solved by sharping the *F* as well, producing a smoother melodic progression, and this form is therefore known as the "melodic" minor scale. Notice that this is done only on the ascending part of the scale, the natural minor being preserved for the descent.

EXTENDED SCALES

For practical use scales of two or more octaves are commonly used, known as "extended" scales. Here is an example of the *C* Major scale in two octaves.

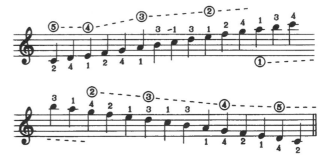

The 2nd finger on the *C* establishes the hand in the 2nd position, which continues until the 1st finger makes a through movement on the 3rd string to play the *C*. This establishes the 5th position for the remainder of the ascending part of the scale. While ascending, left hand fingers remain on the notes after playing until there is a change of string or position. In moving through to change position, the 1st finger does not lose contact with the string.

MAKING THE BEST USE OF SCALES

The scale should first be memorized so that it can readily be incorporated into daily practice. It should be played slowly at first, with particular attention to good left hand position (particularly the 4th finger). With the right hand the various forms of alternation should be used, including those using the *a* finger (*m a m a m a*, etc., or *i a i a i a i a*, etc.). Particular attention should be given to producing an even, clear sound at a good volume with a consistent quality between all the notes. Only when a very clear and accurate scale can be played should the speed be increased. The position changes should be definite and clear in the mind and should be executed with complete smoothness.

SCALE FINGERINGS

Obviously, on the guitar there are many possible alternative ways to finger the scales. The version recommended is that edited by André Segovia,* which includes an example of major and melodic minor scales in all keys.

*Published by Columbia Music Co., Washington, D.C.

THREE STRING SCALES

Some people, this author included, find that extensive alternation on the wound 4th, 5th, and 6th strings can produce a snag in the fingernail at the point of contact. Such a snag impedes smoothness of playing and is hard to eliminate. For this reason, while recognizing the value of scales in all keys, I tend to prefer scales on the first three strings where purely muscular practice is the object. The following is such a scale in the key of *A*, and the same pattern may be used for *A♭*, *B*, and *B♭*.

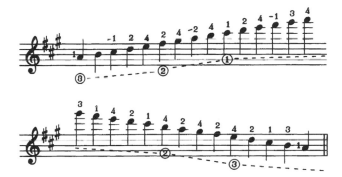

Melody and Arpeggio

In the early stages of learning the guitar, it is possible to abide by simple rules of technique that apply in the majority of cases. For instance, the rest stroke is *usually* employed for scale runs, the free stroke *usually* for arpeggios. However, more advanced studies often require the abandonment of these general rules, a common example being the use of the rest stroke in an arpeggio to emphasize a melody.

RECOGNITION OF MELODY IN ARPEGGIO

Many attractive pieces that have been written for the guitar take the form of a continuous series of arpeggios. Usually one or more notes in each arpeggio group serve a melodic function as well, so that the music is in fact in two lines (i.e., melody and accompaniment), but this is disguised by the fact that the melody note is in a sense shared with the accompaniment. This is best understood by considering the following example:

The melody can be indicated in two ways. In this example it is shown by the tails of the melody notes going upward as well as being joined below to the arpeggio. In some scores the two notes are drawn side by side, but the meaning is exactly the same.

TECHNIQUE FOR EMPHASIS OF MELODY

Wherever possible the melody is "extracted" from the arpeggio by playing it with a rest stroke for emphasis, the remainder of the arpeggio being played conventionally with free strokes.

In practicing this technique, particular care should be taken not to pull the hand back when executing the rest stroke, as this will make the free strokes that follow difficult to play. Take care to avoid any unnecessary movement of the right hand.

Now here is the complete piece.

STUDY NOTES FOR *ETUDE IN B MINOR*
by Fernando Sor (1778–1839)

This study affords the perfect opportunity for extracting a melody from an arpeggio to give the effect of two distinct voices. Use rest strokes for the melody note at the beginning of each measure.

A   The 3rd finger should remain on the *F♯* throughout the first six measures to facilitate the left hand changes. Remember that an arpeggio is a broken chord, and the left hand should prepare complete chords and not individual notes.

B   The 2nd finger is used here so that the 1st remains free in preparation for the bar. Try to make this transition as smooth as possible.

C   The 1st finger has a difficult transition here from the *C* natural, but the alternatives are even more complicated. The secret is not to rush the movement.

D   From here to the end of the piece it is particularly important to make the melody as smooth and lyrical as possible. Extra practice is needed on the change to the fourth position.

E   Leave the 3rd finger on the string so that it can act as a guide down to the second position in the next measure.

Etude in B Minor

Etude in B Minor (continued)

Ornamentation

It is quite common to find music decorated with certain flourishes, which bear the general name of "ornamentation." The subject is a large one since there are many forms of ornament, and their interpretation varies with the period of music. This lesson deals with those in common use in guitar scores.

THE TRILL

The trill is perhaps the commonest form of ornament and may be written in either of the ways shown:

In music of the eighteenth century and earlier, the trill should start on the note above (which may be a whole or half-tone according to the key), and the example should be played thus:

In later music it became the custom to start the trill on the lower note, in this form:

The exact number of notes is less clearly defined in the later trills, the sign calling for a fast repetition of the notes for the length of time of the note over which it is written.

TECHNIQUE OF THE TRILL

Trills are normally played ligado, only the first note being sounded by the right hand. The remaining notes are played by the left hand by a series of clear ascending and descending ligados. When doing this be sure to pull the string firmly to sound the lower note–there is a tendency among students to hammer correctly but just to *take* the finger off instead of *pulling* it off.

An interesting alternative fingering is sometimes used for trills on the 1st string.

In this example after pulling off the 2nd finger the 3rd finger hammers alternating with the 2nd throughout the trill.

THE MORDENT

The sign for the mordent and its explanation are shown next.

Written   Played

It is important to note that the first note is played on the beat, so that in this example a bass note would coincide with the first *F*:

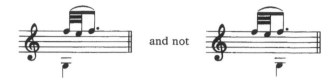 and not

Written   Played

The small note is played very fast and really has no exact time, but effectively "borrows" an instant from the succeeding note. It should be played ligado.

The mordent is common in music of the eighteenth century and earlier. Later the reverse mordent is more common, and the guitarist will encounter many examples of this in Spanish music. As with the trill, only the first note is played by the right hand, the remainder being played ligado by the left hand.

The slow appoggiatura common in eighteenth-century music normally borrows half the time of the succeeding note.

Written   Played

Due to the slower nature of this type of ornament, it requires no special technique.

THE REVERSE MORDENT

There is a distinct trap in the way a reverse mordent is written. Care should be taken to avoid the common misinterpretation of many self-taught students. It is written and played as follows:

Written   Played

The trap is, of course, that the bass note appears to coincide with the second *F*, whereas it is played with the *first* note of the ornament.

THE APPOGGIATURA

The most common form of this ornament that the guitarist will encounter is the "fast" appoggiatura, as follows:

CONCLUSION

The subject of ornamentation is of less importance for the guitarist than for the keyboard player. Music written for the lute and guitar contains fewer and simpler ornaments, and in the case of the lute it is clear from comparison of manuscripts that these were left largely to the individual taste of the player and are unessential to the original composition. The main purpose of studying elaborate ornamentation is to avoid gross errors when playing transcriptions from Bach, Scarlatti, and others. A full treatment of the subject is beyond the scope of this book but will be found in *Solo Guitar Playing*, Book II, where ornamentation is dealt with extensively in the context of different periods of music.

STUDY NOTES FOR *PAVANE IN A MINOR* by Gaspar Sanz (1640–1710)

Gaspar Sanz, a Spanish courtier, developed an important method for the five-course guitar, which was first published in 1674. His themes, which drew on the fanfares and heraldic sounds of the court as well as on popular dances, formed the basis for the *Fantasia Para Un Gentilhombre* concerto for guitar and orchestra by Joaquin Rodrigo.

This *Pavane* is selected from the 1674 method and is full of distinctive and interesting effects.

A Do not be alarmed by the sixteenth notes, which are simply a trill written out in full. The effect is more important than the exact number of notes.

B Although written before the the beat, the fast ornament notes are played on the beat, that is,

Such ornaments are normally slurred, in this case a pull-off followed by a hammer.

C It is possible to sustain the low *B* by using the side of the first finger, as for a bar, on the two *F* sharps that follow. This slightly unorthodox technique is very useful at times.

D Both notes in these groups are done with an upward ligado. It is important to practise these until both hammer strokes can be clearly heard. The final effect is interesting and dramatic.

The overall tempo should be stately and the feeling rather grand.

Pavane

The Seventh Position

THE IMPORTANCE OF HIGHER POSITIONS

It is hard to overemphasize the importance of working toward a thorough knowledge of the fingerboard. Many students of the guitar who have been playing literally for years have only the vaguest knowledge of the higher positions and are afraid to try pieces that are well within their technical capacity because of the reading difficulties.

It is suggested that the studies that follow, which are progressive in difficulty, be used conscientiously as a means of becoming totally familiar with this part of the guitar.

EXERCISE NOTES

Each of the exercises can be played without moving from the seventh position. Exercise 146 is particularly important for becoming familiar with the lower three strings in this area of the guitar. The open *B*, which alternates with each of the other notes, simply adds interest to the exercise and may be ignored while the notes on the lower strings are being worked out.

NOTES IN THE SEVENTH POSITION

Exercise 142

(Elizabethan air)
P. Rosseter

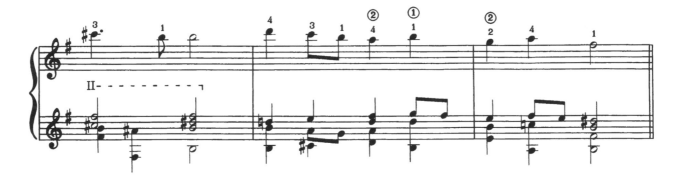

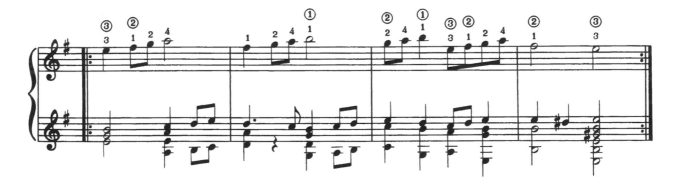

Exercise 143

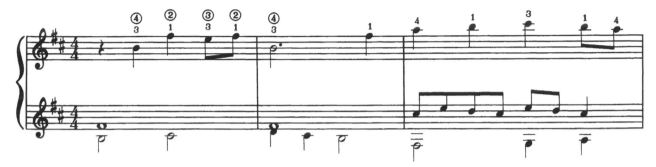

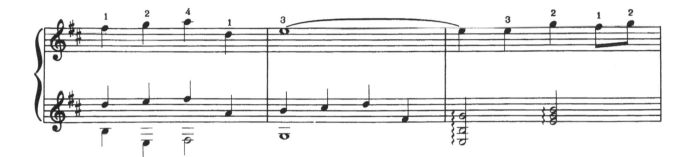

Exercise 144

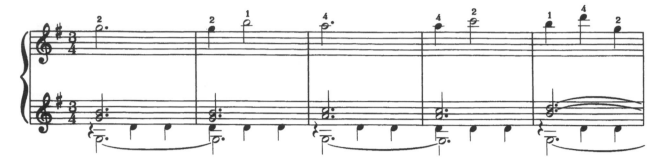

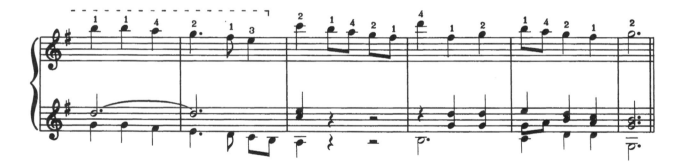

Exercise 145

Exercise 145 (continued)

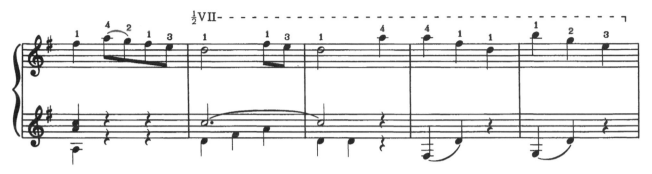

Exercise 146

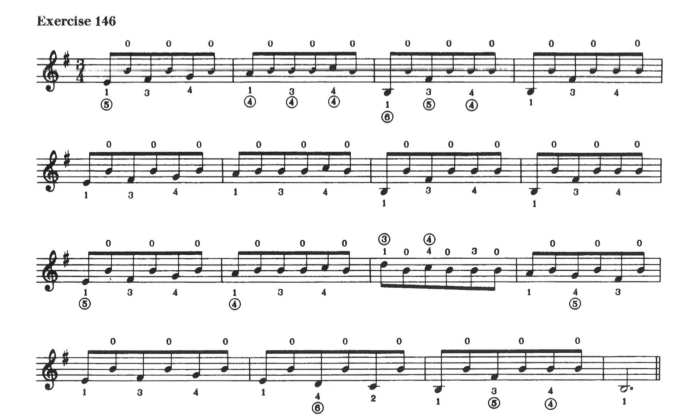

Allegro

FRANZ JOSEPH HAYDN (1732–1809)

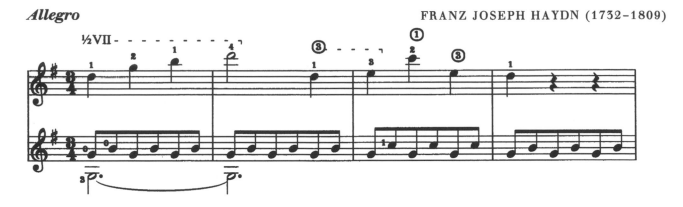

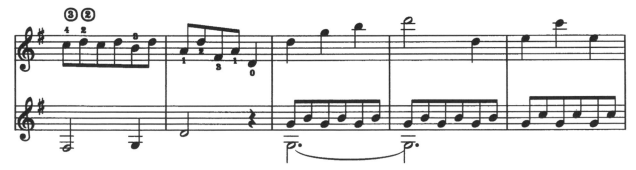

NINE PIECES WITH STUDY NOTES

PRELUDE
by Robert de Visée (1686)

Robert de Visée, a performer of both the guitar and the lute, was a favored chamber musician of Louis XIV. His duties included frequent private performances for the king in addition to participation in the many splendid court occasions.

The guitar was extremely popular both in France and England at this period, the instrument at the time having five pairs of strings tuned in unison or octaves to increase resonance. These pieces are selected from a group published in 1686 and dedicated to the king.

The *Prelude* should be played smoothly at a tempo of about ♩ = 76.

A Make the entry of the second voice clear, sustaining the notes for their full value.

B The position change here is to put the hand in place to take the *A* on the fourth string, so that the entry of this voice has a consistent sound.

C The small note here is a reminder to start the trill on the upper note.

D As in C, the small *D* indicates that the trill starts with the upper note.

ALLEMAND
by Robert de Visée

Allemand, like *Pezzo Tedesco,* means "German" dance. However, by the seventeenth century it was no longer danced, surviving as a stylized musical form in the "Suite." It should be played in moderate tempo, about ♩ = 108.

This is the most difficult of this group of pieces, and the fingering should be carefully observed, in particular the guide finger indications.

A Drop the last joint of the 1st finger to cover the *F.*

B The same fingering as *A.* Lift the last joint slightly to allow the open *E* to sound without releasing the *C.*

C This barred chord is a stretch for the left hand, but it is one to practice as it constantly recurs.

D The *E* has to be found at the 7th fret of the 5th string in order to place the hand in position to commence the repeat.

E Unfortunately it is not possible to sustain the high *A* when the 3rd finger moves to the *A* on the 4th string, but this is a necessary preparation for the next chord.

F This is a particularly hard chord change because of the move from full to half bar. Practice this measure by itself several times.

Allemand

Allemand (continued)

SARABAND
by Robert de Visée

With its dignified slow triple rhythm, the *Saraband* provides a contrast to the quicker dances that follow. It is formed on the early chord sequence known as "la folia," which many seventeenth- and eighteenth-century composers used as the basis for variations.

A simplified first position version was given on page 86, but the piece is offered here in its original key for those who wish to perform these dances as a group.

A Practice is needed here to ensure a smooth transition to the 5th position in the absence of guide fingers.

B The slightly unusual left hand fingering is necessary to ensure a smooth transition to the chord on the first beat of the next measure. I suggest a tempo no faster than ♩= 52.

Saraband

GIGUE
by Robert de Visée

This *Gigue* (*Jig* in English) should be played with sparkle to make a lively conclusion to the four pieces when played together. Aim for a tempo of about ♩ = 168.

A   The hand remains in the fifth position, the open *B* being used to avoid a move. The thumb may be used on the *C♯* to emphasize the entry of the lower voice.

B   As in the prelude at *B* the position change en-

ables the *A* to be taken on the 4th string for a consistent sound in this voice.

C   At this point the 1st finger should be ready to ease through quickly to the third position bar.

D   The second *C* belongs to the lower voice, and this is made clear by taking it on a different string.

E   From here to the end, particular attention should be paid to the left hand fingering. The passage is not difficult if played exactly as written.

F   Place the full bar for the single *F* in preparation for the chord that follows.

Gigue

(continued on next page)

Gigue (continued)

TWO ETUDES
by Matteo Carcassi (1792–1853)

Carcassi was one of the most renowned guitarists of his day, and also a prolific composer. As a supplement to his famous instruction method, he wrote twenty-five studies from which these are selected.

Etude in A

Remember to find the complete chord with both right and left hand at the beginning of each arpeggio group, and follow the pattern of accented notes throughout the piece as indicated in the first three measures.

A   Do not be daunted by this change, which is one of the hardest in the piece. It comes with practice— at first try placing just the 3rd and 4th fingers, then add the other two.

B   The 2nd finger is an important guide for reaching the position.

C   The half bar may remain on or not according to preference.

D   Here also the 2nd finger as a guide takes the difficulty out of the move to the ninth position bar. On a high bar like this be careful not to lift the left elbow—it should remain naturally by your side.

E   Do not be rushed about making this change. In fact a slight pause on the preceding high *D* sounds good musically.

Etude in F

The flat keys tend to be used much less in guitar music due to the associations of the open strings with sharp keys. As a result it becomes a pleasure to find a good piece in a flat key as a change for the ear.

This etude is not hard to play and affords the opportunity to bring out the melody note with rest strokes to achieve the best possible tone. The feeling of the piece is gentle and romantic.

Etude In A

Etude In F

Andante

rit.

MINUET IN C
by Fernando Sor (1778–1839)

Although learning the notes may present some difficulty at first, this is probably the easiest of Sor's minuets and also one of his best. Careful attention to fingering, in particular guide fingers, should result in a rewarding piece to play.

A   All four notes are slurred. Play the *D*, then pull off the 4th finger to sound the *C*. The 1st finger pulls off to sound the open *B*, then hammers down for the final *C*. Be sure to be right on the tip of the 4th finger.

B   A quick movement is needed here to reach the third position bar, but it is preferable to other more complicated fingerings.

C   The small "grace" note has no real time-value and should be pulled off quickly to the *C*.

D   Sound the portamento as the 4th finger travels up to the 10th fret to the *A*. The *F* is beside it, also at the 10th fret.

E   This passage is very easily memorized as the same sequence is repeated in each of the four positions. Try to make quick clear ligados at the beginning of each measure in this passage.

F   Remember that the grace note, although drawn before the chord, must be sounded simultaneously with the *G* and *E*. Then pull off quickly to the *C*.

G   The movement to this chord and the succeeding five measures need extra practice. The fingering is somewhat awkward, but there is no reasonable alternative.

H   Here also the *E* sounds with the *B* and *G* although drawn before the chord. Then the 1st and 4th fingers hammer, and the 4th pulls off to sound the *F*. Try to make the movement rapid and clear.

Minuet in C

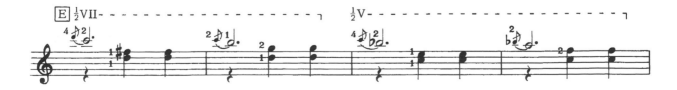

ANDANTINO
by Mauro Giuliani (1781–1829)

This piece serves to introduce another major composer-guitarist of the early nineteenth century, Mauro Giuliani. Of Italian origin, Giuliani settled in Vienna where he met Beethoven and other major musical figures of the period. In England a magazine called *The Giulianiad* was established by loyal fans as a tribute to his contributions.

Much of Giuliani's music has a symphonic flavor that will be recognized in this *Andantino*. It exploits the guitar well but is technically not too difficult.

A This passage should be practiced until there is no feeling of rush. It is important not to slow down the overall tempo when the sixteenths are encountered.

Andantino

ANDANTE
by Dionisio Aguado (1784–1849)

A contemporary and friend of Fernando Sor, Aguado also came from Spain to settle in Paris. Whereas Sor favored short nails for the right hand, Aguado's technique involved playing with the nail as we do today.

Aguado's teaching method was first published in 1825 and contained some delightful short pieces. This romantic *Andante* is one of the best, giving full opportunity for a singing upper melody and expressive dynamics.

A A second dot adds half the value of the previous

dot to the original note. The first dot added an eighth, so the second adds a further sixteenth. It could also be written like this:

B The change of fingers here is in preparation for the reach to the high *C* sharp. Aguado would have stayed in the fifth position, but the instrument of that period had a smaller fingerboard simplifying such stretches.

Andante

Contrapuntal Music

To people unfamiliar with the guitar and its music, one of the most surprising aspects is the ability of the guitarist to play music in which the melodies are in more than one part. A frequent comment is that a good guitarist can sound like two people playing. This illusion comes from the player's careful attention to the different lines or voices in the score and to the time-values of each. For this reason special care should be given to the value of every note.

To stress the equal importance of each melodic line, the following exercises are given in "canon" form, the second voice following the first with the same melody. When a new voice enters, make this clear by giving it slightly extra prominence over the other part. Each line must be sustained exactly as if it were played on a separate instrument. Only after these have been perfected should exercise 149 be attempted.

Exercise 147

Exercise 148

Exercise 148 (continued)

Exercise 149

STUDY NOTES FOR *ETUDE IN C*
by Fernando Sor (1778–1839)

This is a very important study, and its purpose is lost if particular attention is not paid to the value of each note in each of the three parts. For this reason very detailed notes are given for the first section and these should not be ignored.

A   Both *D* and *G* should still be sounding clearly with the *B*.

B   As you play the 4th string *E* the 2nd finger must still remain on the C♯.

C   Both *D* and *F* must ring through to the end of the measure.

D   The 3rd finger remains firmly placed until it moves up to the *G*.

E   Similarly the 1st finger holds the *E* until it has to transfer to the *C*. This fingering enables the *C* and *A* to be sustained for the remainder of the mea-

sure. Note that in this and the succeeding measure, where the lower voice moves, the other two are sustained and vice versa. Try to make this clearly audible by playing the sustained notes strongly enough to sound through.

F   Give emphasis to the entry of the lower voice here and to that of the upper voice in the next measure.

G   Leave the 2nd finger on the *F* when you reach for the high *A*.

H   The upper notes must sound through the complete measure.

I   To bring out and help sustain the tied notes, the chords on the third beat of this and the succeeding measures may be arpeggiated slightly. As the upper note of the chord is reached, the right hand finger gives a slight extra pull to this string.

J   Remember to leave the 4th finger on in preparation for the grace note in the final measure.

Etude in C

Harmonics

NATURAL HARMONICS

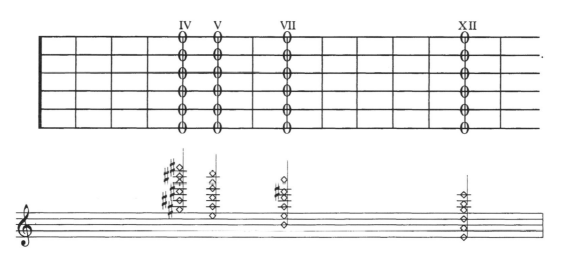

Harmonic notes available at the 4th, 5th, 7th, and 12th frets.

The available notes in succession. The upper note represents the sound in guitar notation, the lower in actual pitch.

A particularly pleasing type of note can be produced by making a string vibrate in sections of its length instead of as a whole. Such notes are known as *harmonics.*

NATURAL HARMONICS

Natural harmonics are produced by touching a string lightly with the left hand at a certain point, playing the string with the right hand, and then immediately taking the left hand away. As a practical example try the following:

1. Touch the 6th string lightly with the 4th finger of the left hand immediately above the 12th fret. The string does not need to be depressed–it is sufficient that the finger is in contact with it.

2. Play this with the right hand thumb slightly more toward the bridge than usual.

3. Immediately take away the left hand finger. A bell-like *E,* an octave above the open string, should continue sounding. In fact the whole length of the string is vibrating, but in two loops divided at the point where the string is touched.

After experimenting until a clear sound is produced, try the same thing on the other strings, in each case touching with the left hand just over the 12th fret. The thumb was used initially because it gives a strong vibration to the string. However, when you are hearing clear harmonics you may experiment with other right hand fingers. Try to make the string vibrate as far as possible in a plane vertical to the fingerboard.

Harmonics may also be produced at the 7th fret, weaker ones at the 5th fret, and in rare cases the 4th fret or even the 3rd fret is used. Here is an example of how natural harmonics are written, and the sounds actually produced:

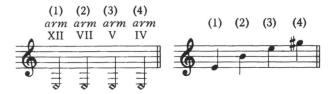

The diamond shape indicates that a harmonic is to be played, as does the abbreviation *arm* (*armonico*). The Roman numeral indicates the fret where the left hand is to touch.

Exercise 150

OCTAVE HARMONICS
(*Armonicos Octavados*)

Octave harmonics, also known as artificial harmonics, are produced by touching a string with the right hand *i* finger at a distance of 12 frets above any note stopped by the left hand. The harmonic is then played with the *a* finger of the right hand. The accompanying photograph shows the position of the hand.

The movement is best illustrated by a practical example:

To play this measure use the following procedure:

1. First find the *F* with the left hand 1st finger.
2. With the right hand index finger, in the position illustrated, touch the string above fret 12, higher than the left hand note, in this case the 13th fret.
3. Pluck the string with the *a* finger, making sure that the *i* finger maintains its contact. Immediately after playing remove the *i* finger from the string.
4. To continue, find the *G* with the left hand 3rd finger. With the right hand index finger touch above the 15th fret (3 + 12). Play as in step 3.
5. Return to the 1st and 15th frets to play the final *F*.

As practice try playing the melodies of exercises 16 to 20 using octave harmonics.

HARMONICS
WITH CHORDS

Since only the *i* and *a* fingers are used by the right hand, it is possible to play two- and even three-note chords with the upper note an octave harmonic.

To execute this example, the left hand first finds the chord. Then with the index finger of the right hand touching the 13th fret, the *a*, *m*, and *p* play respectively the 1st, 3rd, and 4th strings together to sound the chord. Although difficult at first, this is one of the most interesting and surprising effects on the guitar.

As practice try playing exercises 71 and 72 with the upper notes in octave harmonics.

Advanced Techniques and Effects

THE TREMOLO

The guitar is not a "sustaining" instrument in that it is not possible to produce a long continuous note as with a bowed instrument or organ. However, it is possible to give the illusion of sustained sound by playing a very fast succession of strokes to repeat a note by the technique known as *tremolo*.

The most common form of tremolo employs the thumb to play a bass or accompaniment part, while each note of the melody is played three times by the *a, m,* and *i* fingers in that order. Here is an example:

To conserve space the tremolo may be written as in the third measure of this example with exactly the same time value and meaning.

TECHNIQUE FOR TREMOLO

The *a, m,* and *i* fingers must of course play free strokes. In general, the thumb should play free strokes too, but occasionally a rest stroke may be used to give emphasis to the first note of a measure.

The fingers should be close together and should use the minimum possible movement, particularly when playing on an inside string. If care is not taken in this respect, the *a* finger will catch the string above.

It is a good idea to practice the right hand technique by itself, taking a simple chord for the left hand, as for instance in the first measure of the example. Repeat the pattern many times starting very slowly and keeping the knuckle part of the right hand absolutely steady.

Increasing Speed

The tremolo is one technique that really does depend on rapid execution for effectiveness. The line of notes does not sound continuous at speeds below $\quarternote = 138$, and some performers can produce an incredible $\quarternote = 176$. To give rules for increasing speed is very difficult since what is effective for one person is not always useful to another. As a result several suggestions are offered for experimentation, in the hope that at least one of them will help.

Slow Practice

It seems strange that slow practice should help the attainment of greater speed, but the fact has been stated and restated by musicians and teachers. What seems to happen is that a very positive and accurate habit is formed, so that there is no vagueness or uncertainty when the movement is played at a faster speed. A suggested way to practice a passage would be to play it four times slowly, then once fast.

Overemphasis of Strokes

This method entails playing the passage at moderate speed, but exaggerating each stroke so that more than usual strength is used. This also produces maximum volume. After playing this way a few times, the hand is relaxed to the normal level, and the passage played with reduced volume and higher speed.

Use of the Metronome

The use of a metronome is interesting in that it gives an exact measure of progress as a passage is worked through. A suggested procedure is to play first at a comfortable speed at which complete accuracy can be guaranteed. Then the metronome is advanced two points, and an attempt is made at the higher speed. Finally the metronome is moved back one point, at which speed complete accuracy is again attempted.

Throughout the study of the tremolo, it should be realized the smooth execution of this technique is closely linked with the control of the *a* finger. For this reason it is often beneficial to "prepare" this finger by playing alternating *m* and *a* and also the reverse arpeggio (*p a m i*).

Further study of the tremolo is beyond the scope of this book but appears in *Solo Guitar Playing,* Book II, which also includes the complete score of Francisco Tárrega's famous tremolo study *Recuerdos de la Alhambra.*

PIZZICATO (*Etouffé*)

The term *pizzicato* is normally applied to the plucking of the strings of instruments that are usually bowed, such as the violin. As the sound produced is somewhat brief and lacking in resonance, the term is borrowed by guitarists to describe a technique whereby notes are played by the thumb,

while the side of the hand rests just behind the bridgebone to act as a mute.

The picture illustrates the position for the right hand. The left hand can add to the effect by releasing each note the instant it has been played by the right hand thumb.

The pizzicato is normally indicated by the abbreviation *pizz* at the beginning of the passage, the individual notes being marked with a dot above or below, as for staccato playing.

TAMBOR

This is a rather rare technique intended to give a drumlike effect. The strings are struck by the side of the thumb very close to the bridgebone. This produces a booming sound through which the resonance of the strings can be heard. The right hand should be held just over the bridge with the muscles completely loose, so that as the side of the thumb strikes the strings, it will immediately rebound from them to avoid muting the sound.

Completion of the Fingerboard

It is not possible in the present work to give detailed exercises and study material in all the positions of the guitar. However, the work continues logically in *Solo Guitar Playing*, Book II, which contains extensive exercises and practice studies in the higher positions.

Although the best study of the fingerboard lies in mastering the positions one by one, there are certain additional aids to memorizing the notes, and some suggestions are offered here.

LEARNING BY EQUIVALENT NOTES

Since one of the difficulties of the guitar is the fact that the same note may appear in so many different places, it is a good idea to make a conscious effort to memorize these equivalents. This is something that can be done away from the instrument and has proved surprisingly successful for some students. Starting at the open *A* the procedure is to "think" through all the notes of the first position and work out mentally where else they occur on the guitar. This mental effort will reveal certain patterns and relationships on the fingerboard, for instance the fact that except between the 2nd and 3rd strings an equivalent note can be found by going down one string and adding 5 to the fret number of the original note. For instance, the *F* at the 1st fret of the 1st string recurs at the 6th (5 + 1) fret of the 2nd string.

LEARNING BY FRET

In the same way that the notes on the staff are learned more easily by separating the lines from the spaces, so the notes on the guitar are better memorized by learning across the frets. To try to learn from scales is more difficult because the succession of notes is in alphabetical order an therefore easy to name without really making a conscious effort at memorization. Again this method may be used away from the guitar, for instance by choosing one fret each day and on repeated occasions visualizing mentally what the notes look like on paper and what their letters are.

TRANSFER OF POSITION

It is a good idea to explore the possibilities of the guitar by making a simple melodic line and trying to play it in as many positions as possible, remaining within the position each time. This not only helps note learning, but also reveals what positions are suitable or more adapted to a given key. It is important therefore to experiment in varied keys, although the melody may be simple.

VARIED READING

There is no better or pleasanter way to learn the fingerboard than by acquiring the habit of reading through collections and anthologies daily. There is the pleasure of discovering a really good piece for further study, and the additional satisfaction of finding that what looked impossible two months ago has now become quite comprehensible. Yet of all the methods it is the one least followed by students, partly through lack of available material and partly because of the greater effort necessary initially, before the rewarding stage is reached. One can only emphasize that work in this direction is amply repaid in the long run.

The duet that follows, *Aria* by Domenico Scarlatti, is transcribed from a keyboard original and provides a pleasant vehicle for exploring the higher positions. For additional material, the student is referred to *Solo Guitar Playing*, Book II, which continues the progress of fingerboard mastery.

Aria

DOMENICO SCARLATTI (1685–1757)

Aria (continued)

CONCLUSION

Whatever the method employed, it is obvious that a knowledge of where the notes are on an instrument is absolutely basic to any serious study of it. The piano student knows where all the notes are on his or her instrument in a matter of hours or days, yet guitar students persistently extend this into months and years. Consequently guitarists tend to lag in musicianship behind other instrumentalists. If you can overcome this pitfall, you will have taken a significant step forward and ahead of the vast majority of students of the guitar.

And now, for your enjoyment and instruction, here are four of the most popular pieces ever written for the guitar.

FOUR PIECES WITH STUDY NOTES

ADELITA
by Francisco Tárrega (1852–1909)

This is another beautiful and lyrical piece. Although called a Mazurka, which is a Polish dance, it is usually played with a moderate flowing tempo.

The second half presents somewhat more technical difficulty than the first, principally because of the ornamentation. If the notes are first learned without the ornaments, be sure to follow the correct fingering so that they may be easily added later without refingering.

A Use vibrato on the high *E,* and make the ligado as smooth as possible.

B Remember that the *first* note of the ornament sounds simultaneously with the low *E.*

C Sound the portamento as the 3rd finger travels down to the *E.*

D   Here also the portamento is effective as the 4th finger moves up the string.

E   The 3rd finger moves down here to put the hand in position for the next chord. In effect this means that the quarter notes cannot be sustained, but up to tempo this is barely noticeable, and the overall result is a much smoother change.

F   The high *G*♯ at the 13th fret may be sounded

without the right hand by the force of the left hand slide.

G   Place the complete bar for the *D*♯ in preparation for the chord that follows.

In general, try not to be deterred by the unfamiliar positions of some of the notes, which are designed to produce the best possible sound from the guitar.

Adelita

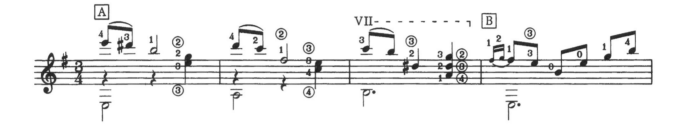

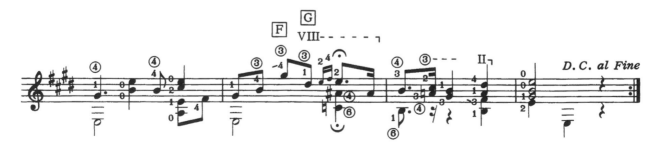

LÁGRIMA
by Francisco Tárrega

Tárrega was one of the most important contributors to the technique and repertoire of the guitar. He is said to have played with a most beautiful and completely individual tone, and the structure of his compositions and transcriptions shows a complete mastery of the instrument. A great teacher also, he is considered one of those principally responsible for the modern recognition of the capabilities of the "classical" guitar.

This piece is romantic in style–"lágrima" means a *teardrop*. The melody should be brought out with rest strokes and every effort should be made to attain smooth continuity.

A   The open *B*'s in the first measure and this group of eighth notes are not part of the melody and should be subdued in relation to the notes with the tails up.

B   The half bars in this measure require practice. Be sure that the finger is pressing evenly across the four strings and not arched. The 3rd finger must be as vertical as possible to avoid muting the third string.

C   This is a typical Tárrega fingering. The hand does not change position, in spite of the open string, until the 4th finger slides up to take the *G*♯ at the 13th fret of the 3rd string. Here the 4th finger must be right on its tip so that the adjacent open string can sound.

D   Leave the hand over the fifth position while playing the open strings in preparation for the *F*♯ at the 7th fret.

Lágrima

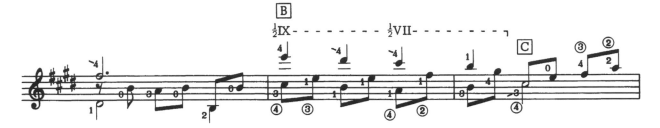

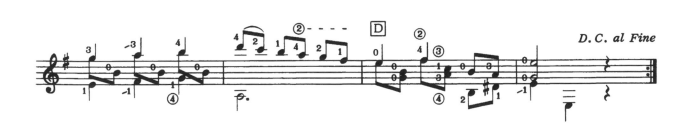

ROMANCE
Anonymous

This is one of the most popular of all pieces for the guitar. It has a simple but haunting melody and should be played at a moderate tempo, bringing out the melody notes. Vibrato is effective if not used to excess.

A Although a half bar would be possible here, the full bar makes the transition to the seventh position easier.

B This stretch out of the position is very hard at first, but becomes much easier when the piece is played up to tempo.

C The barred positions in the second half of the piece are more difficult than those previously encountered because of the length of time that they must be held. It is important not to strain the left hand by doing too much at once. Never force the left hand–lay the fingers out flat and rest the hand at the first sign of any discomfort. This will achieve more than will a grim determination to continue.

From its sound this is always supposed to be a fairly easy piece. In fact it needs considerable practice, but this will result in a strengthening and general improvement of the left hand.

Romance

Romance (continued)

EL TESTAMEN DE N'AMELIA
by Miguel Llobet (1878–1939)

Llobet was one of Tárrega's most distinguished pupils. He had a successful concert career, and although he wrote few original works he made a number of fine arrangements somewhat in the style of Tárrega.

This piece is an arrangement of a popular Catalonian folk song. Although perhaps beyond the scope of this book, it is offered because of its particular beauty for those ambitious enough to try it.

A   These natural harmonics can all be taken with the 3rd finger. Remember that the finger does not have to touch with its tip, the underneath part of the extended finger being sufficient to stop the string for the harmonic.

B   The octave harmonic section should be taken in three stages. First, memorize thoroughly the left hand movements playing the passage *without* harmonics. Then practice the melody, only forming the octave harmonics. Finally complete the passage by adding the accompaniment.

C   For contrast the melody now lies on the fourth string. These notes should be brought out strongly with the chords somewhat subdued as accompaniment.

El Testamen de N'amelia

6th string to D

Andante expresivo

Music for Guitar Ensemble

A NOTE TO THE TEACHER

As far as possible the trios and quartets that follow have been arranged with sufficient simplicity to supplement the earlier lessons in the book. However, it is impossible to achieve much musical effect with all parts in the 1st position, and it will be found that the upper voice must often go to the 5th fret and above. Rather than waiting until the whole class has learned the higher notes, the 1st parts may initially be taken by the teacher, or as occurs in most classes, by the one or two participants who are ahead of the main group.

In cases where the bass part is in two lines these can easily be initially divided between two groups and later used for the practice of simple chords.

The final selection, *Trio Facile Pour Trois Guitares,* by the early nineteenth-century composer Leonhard von Call, is as the title states, an original work for three guitars. It is remarkable in combining simplicity with considerable musical charm and affords the student an extended work where the focus can be on expression and dynamics rather than simply finding the notes. It was purposely left unfingered (as published) so as to leave room for experimentation. I have personally had excellent results from the *Trio Facile* and strongly recommend it to other teachers.

Song Tune   THOMAS CAMPIAN (1567–1620)

Bourrée

G. F. HANDEL (1685–1759)

Minuet

G. F. HANDEL (1685–1759)

Minuet (continued)

Gavot

G. F. HANDEL (1685–1759)

Gavot (continued)

Gavot   G. F. HANDEL (1685–1759)

Awake Sweet Love   JOHN DOWLAND (1563–1626)

Mrs. Nichols' Almain

Mrs. Nichols' Almain (continued)

Courant

ANONYMOUS*

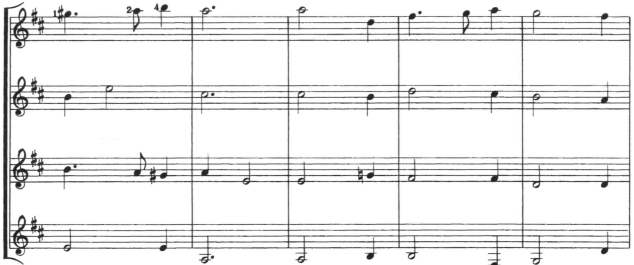

*From _Terpsichore_ (1612), compiled by Michael Praetorius

Courant (continued)

Ballet
ANONYMOUS*

*From *Terpsichore* (1612), compiled by Michael Praetorius

Ballet (continued)

Largo

ANTONIO VIVALDI (*c.* 1676–1741)

Largo (continued)

Minuet

JOSEF HAYDN (1732–1809)

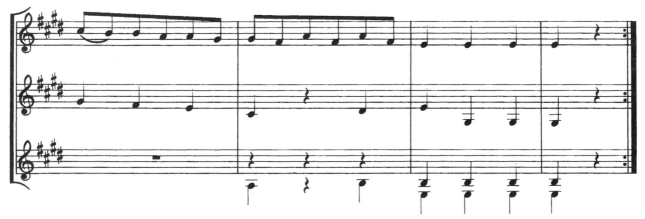

Minuet (continued)

Grave

G. P. TELEMANN (1681–1767)

Grave (continued)

Chorale

J. S. BACH (1685–1750)

Trio Facile Pour Trois Guitares

LEONHARD VON CALL

ADAGIO 1

Trio Facile Pour Trois Guitares (continued)

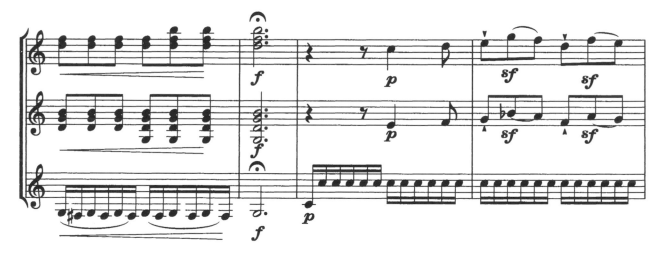

Trio Facile Pour Trois Guitares (continued)

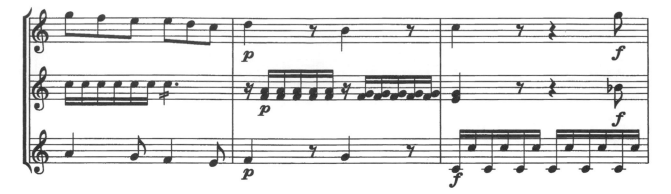

MINUET

Trio Facile Pour Trois Guitares (continued)

Trio

Trio Facile Pour Trois Guitares (continued)

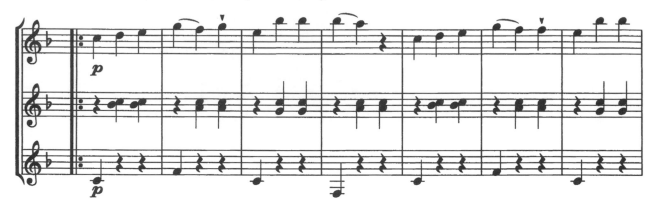

Minuet D.C.

Trio Facile Pour Trois Guitares (continued)

ADAGIO 2

Leonhard von Call

Trio Facile Pour Trois Guitares (continued)

RONDO

Leonhard von Call

Trio Facile Pour Trois Guitares (continued)

Trio Facile Pour Trois Guitares (continued)

WILSON'S WILDE
Anonymous

This piece is from the Dowland lute book. Although easy to play, it is a very effective composition because of the amount of variety in a simple framework.

Each of three themes is followed by an ornamented repeat; if the themes are treated with a sustained quality, the repeats may be given an interesting contrast by being played with a brisk attack. Suggested tempo is ♩ = 152.

Wilson's Wilde

LESSON FOR TWO LUTES
Anonymous

A comfortable andante tempo is suggested, about ♩ = 88.

Taken from the same manuscript as the preceding piece, this delightful but simple duet should present no technical difficulties if the fingering is strictly followed.

Lesson for Two Lutes

ALMAN
by Robert Johnson

The manuscripts contain much solo music of both Robert Johnson (who also wrote many songs) and of his father, John. Robert's music is characteristically simpler and more melodic than the sophisticated compositions of his father. The word *Alman* is the same as *Allemande*, or "German" (dance).

Suggested tempo is ♩ = 108.

1. *It is important to place the full bar down for the* F♯, *which takes the difficulty out of the fast change.*

Alman

BOURRÉE
by J. S. Bach

Among the instruments in Bach's collection listed after his death were two lutes and a mechanical instrument known as a *Lautenwerk*. The latter was a form of harpsichord designed by Bach and made for him by the organ builder Zacharias Hildebrand which imitated very exactly the sound of the lute. It is reasonable to suppose that Bach had a working knowledge of the lute, but in view of the difficulty of playing the instrument well on a part-time basis he may have preferred the ease of the keyboard imitation. It is certain that he enjoyed the lute, and when Wilhelm Friedman Bach brought the lutenists S. L. Weiss and

J. Kropfgans to see him in July of 1739 it was reported that "something special in the way of music" occurred.

The bourrée below, a most popular piece for guitarists, is from the Suite in E Minor (BWV 996). It occurs in a collection made by Bach's pupil Johann Ludwig Krebs in two staff notation, and a later hand added the words "aufs Lautenwerk."

Suggested tempo is a lively ♩ = 120, and care should be taken to sustain this tempo through the last four or five measures which are slightly more complex than the rest of the piece.

Although by Bach's time the bourrée had become a stylized movement of the baroque suite, it seems to retain the flavor of its origin as a robust French provincial peasant dance.

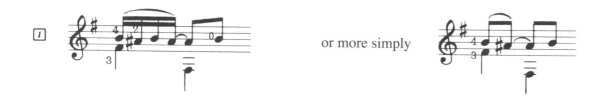

or more simply

2 *Note the change of position here, with the B on the sixth string.*

Baroque music printing. Title page of *Frische Clavier Früchte* by Johann Kuhnau

Bourrée

CANARIOS
by Gaspar Sanz

One of the interesting treatises on the guitar of the seventeenth century is that of Gaspar Sanz, who describes himself as from the province of Aragon and a bachelor of theology of the University of Salamanca. The book was published in 1674 in Zaragoza with the title *Instrucción de Musica Sobre la Guitarra Española*, and contains detailed instructions in technique as well as many musical examples of the dance forms popular in Spain such as *Folios*, *Españoletas*, *Rujeros* and the *Canarios* transcribed below.

As with most music written for the baroque guitar it is impossible to re-create the original in a transcription, but the particularly Spanish charm of the dance comes through nevertheless.

[1] *The occasional ¾ interspersed with the § is particularly Spanish and rhythmically interesting and effective.*

[2] *Note the change from fourth to third finger on the A, necessary for what follows.*

The double bars at the end of each section may be taken as optional, rather than essential, repeats.

Suggested tempo for the dance is ♩. = 112.

Canarios

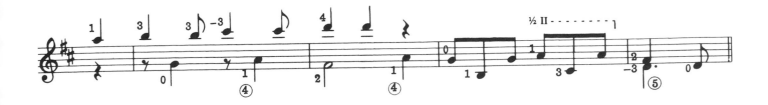

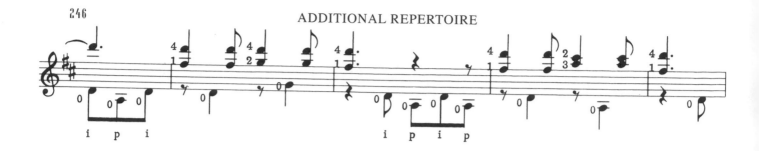

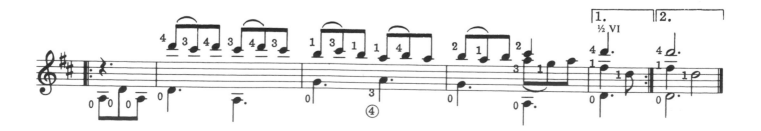

THEME FROM OP. 102
by Mauro Giuliani

Guitar arrangements of operatic solos were extremely popular in the early nineteenth century. This example is from the opera *Baccanali di Roma* by Generali, and is an arrangement of a Cavatina. It was first published by Diabelli, the complete work comprising

Introduction, Theme and Variations, and also appeared as a quartet with guitar. The theme was reprinted in the English magazine for guitar enthusiasts *The Giulianiad* (1833–1835).

1 *The hammer with the third finger is awkward, but it comes on a weak beat so there is no need to apply excessive force.*

Suggested tempo ♩ = 88.

Theme from Op. 102

CAPRICE OP. 20, NO. 2
by Luigi Legnani (1790–1877)

Legnani is perhaps best known as a close friend and associate of Paganini, with whom he gave a number of concerts. He was a prolific composer, with published works exceeding two hundred and fifty for solo guitar and small instrumental combinations, and he enjoyed a wide reputation as a virtuoso performer.

The *Caprice* is chosen from a series in all keys designed for technique development.

1. *In the original the B is slurred to the E— possible on the smaller fingerboard of the nineteenth century guitar, but here re-fingered for the modern instrument.*

2. *Although this passage may appear complicated, it is in fact simple as the same diminished chord is moved down through the various positions.*

Suggested tempo ♩ = 76.

Caprice Op. 20, No. 2

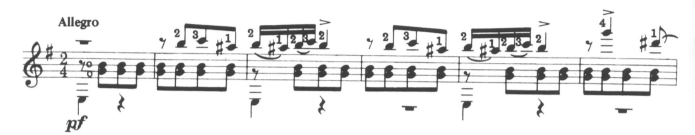

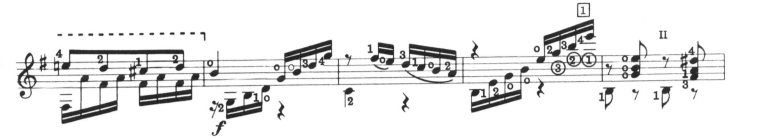

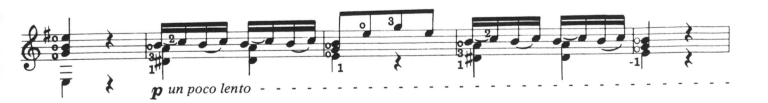

NOCTURNE OP. 4, NO. 2
by Johann Kaspar Mertz (1806–1856)

The Austrian J. K. Mertz was one of the leading figures in Europe to maintain interest in the guitar after the era of Sor and Giuliani (see Introduction). In the early part of this century the American teacher George Krick wrote "While wandering through the streets of old historic Vienna, and seeing monuments that had been erected to Mozart, Beethoven and other grand old masters, I wondered if it were possible that such a city could have forgotten Mertz, who performed for their princes and nobility, and who dedicated many of his compositions and arrangements to their names... but yet it was so, and even they who had published his music could only give an approximate guess as to the date of his death," George Krick's collection now resides in the Gaylord Music Library at Washington University, St. Louis, Missouri, and contains a large resource of Mertz's publications including this simple *Nocturne* from one of his early works.

Nocturne Op. 4, No. 2

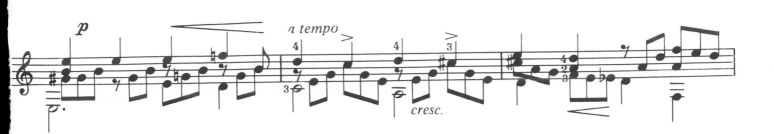

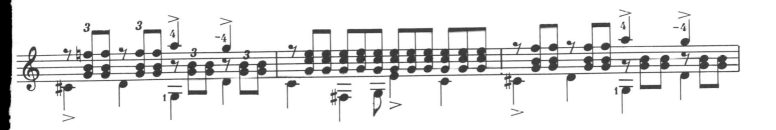

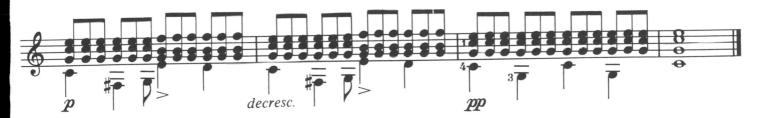

Two Pieces from
RÉCRÉATION DU GUITARISTE, OP. 51
by Napoleon Coste (1806–1883)

Napoleon Coste was a pupil of Fernando Sor, and like Sor wrote a number of simple but attractive pieces for beginners in addition to his more ambitious works.

The Opus 51 collection was known as the *Récréation du Guitariste*. The *Rondeau* and *Barcarolle* are included here. A *barcarolle* imitates the song of a Venetian gondolier.

Rondeau, Op. 51, No. 6

Barcarolle, Op. 51, No. 1

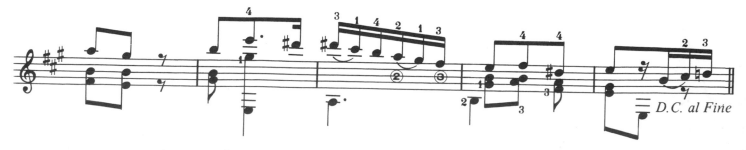